POWERSPELLS

P⊕WERSPELLS

Get the Magical Edge
in Business,
Work Relationships,
and Life

Lexa Roséan

St. Martin's Griffin ♒ New York

www.stmartins.com

ISBN 0-312-27476-9

First Edition: October 2001

10 9 8 7 6 5 4 3 2 1

For
Tracy Morgan

C⊕N✝EN✝S

ACKNOWLEDGMENTS

Thank you all for your inspiration, information,
nurturing, and support

Akis Petroulas

Alfonso Ramirez

Balducci's, Chelsea Market, C-Town, Key Food

Garden of Eden & Gristedes

Cynthia Nudelman

Easyenchantments.com

El Gordo, El Flaco, y La Llorona

El Pulpo

Elvira

Garbo 180

Heidi Griffiths

Helen Eisenbach

Jen Enderlin

Joel and Priscilla

Jordan Thaler

Juan Pablo

La Bicha

La Bicha

La Bicha, *Muchas gracias por todo, no sabes cuanto significas para mí.*

Lisa Hagen

Mamy

Matthew Sawicki

Meryl

Nasim Alikani

Nicklausse

Regine

Robert Waife

Sandra Martin

Sharon, Reneè, Gigi, and Jessica Brauner

Steven Schatzman

Tomas Reale

the Goddess

the Naugahyde chair

★ special thanks to my automatic writing partners
Alina Troyano and Madeleine Olnek
and to Loreen Arbus (my closest friend and muse)
. . . without you three I would never write
you made me love it or at least DO IT when I hated it most . . .
thank you from the bottom of my big fat Mont Blanc babies!

IN✛R⊕DUC✛I⊕N

I would like to begin with some words on spells. Spells are meant to be used in conjunction with real action to obtain our goals. They are not, as many would use them, a last-ditch effort to get what we want when all other methods have failed. They are not a way to circumvent getting our hands dirty. They are not about twitching the nose like Samantha Stevens to command the mess of our lives to fall into place, one-two-three alakazam. No, sir. No, ma'am. Most of us, especially when dealing with our careers, which belong to the material world, forget to build our spiritual or magical muscles as well. This is what spells are for. You cannot expect to succeed and fulfill your true potential without honoring and calling forth the divine aspect within yourself. It raises everything to another level. Spells when used in this capacity summon serendipity.

The most frequently asked questions about spells are "Do they work?" and "How do they work?" I must answer the second question before I can answer the first. Spells work on three different levels. The first is as a form of prayer. In most ancient civilizations food was offered to the gods to win their favor. The summoning of divine energy, blessing, and assistance into all undertakings was considered crucial. Witches still honor this sacred tradition. You will find many spells that require you to leave an offering to a particular deity, or to work with a certain substance that is sacred to that deity in order to draw the energy of that particular god or goddess to help you fulfill your goal. If this type of spell does not work, we must ask ourselves why it is that some prayers are answered and others are not. I could speculate forever upon the possibilities, but truly this answer lies in the hands of the gods.

The second reason spells are effective is because the ingredients themselves hold magical properties or energies. Every plant, food, herb, spice, everything under the sun and moon has an astrological sign, just like you and me. This sign gives that substance predictable characteristics. Many herbs and foods also have mythological lore associated with them and a historical tradition of magical use. It is with this combined knowledge that I formulate my spells. Tapping into the spiritual vibrations that the ingredients contain will help you create specific effects. I will give you two examples to illustrate my point. Milk contains calcium. No one will argue that fact. If I tell you that milk contains the spiritual quality of nurturing, you will probably agree as well. All of us can easily conjure up the image of mothers' milk nurturing the suckling babe. Now, if I tell you that oranges contain vitamin C, you will also agree. But you may raise an eyebrow or two when I tell you that oranges contain the spiritual vibration of love. This is probably something you are not as familiar with. The orange blossom, because it was given by Jove to the goddess Juno on their wedding day, has become a universal flower symbolic of matrimonial love. This energy extends to the fruit of the blossom as well. Witches recognize and accept these spiritual qualities right along with the nutritional ones. The study of aromatherapy has also lent some scientific validity to the way the properties of essences can affect the brain.

This now brings me to the third explanation of how spells work. The ingredients are keys to unlock and direct the subconscious will. They symbolize your internal power and connection with the divine. The combination of the second and third principles of operation are what really give spells their drive. The ingredients hold properties or energies on their own. When you imbue a food or magical item with your intent, it becomes doubly powerful. For example, a VCR or a power notebook holds a great deal of potential. But when you program that VCR to tape your favorite TV show or when you link your power book up to a modem or CD ROM you fulfill its potential and make the machine work for you to fulfill your needs. Spells are the same.

If something does not work based on these two principles, it is because you have chosen a spell with ingredients that your subconscious will does not respond to, or ingredients that do not really match your desired goal. I have included a variety of ways to achieve the same magical end within this book. (Notice the similarity between Accomplishment of Tasks spell and spell to Get Motivated.) There are many remedies and potions for a variety of work-related matters. Some are potions to be rubbed into the hands and skin, or sprinkled, some are baths to be taken, offerings to be left to deities, others involve the making of magical talismans to be worn or ingested. All are powerful forms of magic. You will have to determine which works best for you. Each individual responds in their own magical way. There are hundreds (maybe thousands) of traditional recipes for success or money, just as there are different varieties of pharmaceuticals to treat various illnesses. Some patients respond well to one drug, while others do not. It is the same with magical spells. A secret to success is to use what you are intuitively drawn to. If the spell does not work, you might also want to analyze your feelings around this particular request or your approach to it. For example, a client of mine saw no results with her numerous success spells. Finally it dawned on her that she was deeply afraid of success. She did the spell to Banish Fear of Success and then went on to repeat the original spells. It was only then that she saw results.

Another frequently asked question is "Do I have to believe in the spell for it to work?" I recently read in the *Wall Street Journal* that most millionaires do not believe in astrology. However, the majority of billionaires do. I think that about sums it up! Faith goes a long way. Especially faith in yourself and the object or goal of your desire. Why ask for something if you don't really want it or believe you deserve it? If you are going to work a spell, commit yourself to it. As with all things in life, the results are more outstanding when we believe in what we are doing.

"Do I have to be a witch to perform a spell?" Hmm... Do you have to be a Mozart to play the piano? No, of course not! Anyone can learn to work a spell. Throughout history, people of all faiths came to consult the old woman in the woods or the local shaman and were given magical advice or potions and concoctions to heal and deal with their lives. Witchcraft, the old religion, dates back to pre-patriarchal times. All the patriarchal religions have elements of the matriarchy buried within them. In a way, no matter what your faith, using witchcraft is just a way of getting back to your roots. Connecting with Mother Nature, the goddess of the earth.

You will notice that the ingredients in these PowerSpells are all easily obtainable. You probably already have many ingredients on your kitchen shelves. The rest are as close as the local market. Many people think the spells will not be as powerful unless they contain strange and exotic items like the ones listed in ancient spellbooks. I hate to disappoint you dear reader but that eye of newt was no more than a nickname for a common marshberry. What you must keep in mind is that some of those bizarre ingredients were readily obtainable to the magicians of old. They were growing right outside their caves. Everything they used in their magic they also used in their daily lives. They found the power in the ordinary and so must we. There are still schools of magical thought that believe in the power of the arcane. My tradition and my teachings are more Zen in their approach. Sometimes the most complex is found within the simplest of things. Kitchen witchery is as old as the hearth. It is very, very powerful!! Perform all the spells as directed. Have confidence and visualize your desired end as clearly as possible for optimum success.

May the gods grant you favors. May the magical properties of everyday things ignite your will and give you the magical edge you need to fulfill your dreams and desires.

Finally and humbly I speak to those cauldron-carrying members of the craft of the wise. I hope I can teach you a few new tricks. Blessèd be.

POWERSPELLS

ACCOMPLISHMENT OF TASKS

INGREDIENTS

drip coffeemaker with filters
or espresso machine and a coffee tamper
dark roast blend of coffee
a pen

This spell is used to brew up some ambition for accomplishing all those work tasks you've been putting off until mañana. Fill your espresso machine with enough water and coffee to brew a shot of espresso. Using a tamper, tamp the coffee down into the filter while speaking out loud the tasks you need to accomplish. Be sure to pack the coffee down tight with the tamper. Also be firm and clear as you announce your tasks. Brew the coffee, add milk and/or sugar or lemon peel depending on your preference, and drink. This ritual should be done right before you set about accomplishing your tasks.

The alternative method is performed with a drip coffeepot or machine that takes paper filters. Using a pen with indelible ink, write your tasks clearly on the paper filter. Place the filter in the machine or pot and fill with coffee. Add water and brew. Season to taste and drink.

Coffee is sacred to Mars and is used to create motivation, stimulate activity, energy, and movement. If you cannot drink coffee, you may add this mixture to your bathwater and immerse yourself in the tub for a minimum of ten minutes. For maximum motivation, use two shots of straight espresso without seasoning. The darker and richer the blend, the more intense your level of concentration will be. Using milk will help to nurture you through your task. However too much milk can slow down the force of Mars. Sugar will sweeten the task. Lemon helps to remove any obstacles in the way of accomplishing your tasks.

ADVANCEMENT: GAINING HONOR, RESPECT, OR RECOGNITION

INGREDIENTS

a medal
cinnamon
bay leaf
yellow silk

Sometimes it's not about the money but rather the recognition. Without building the reputation you cannot make the money. Once you are known and have established yourself and your credibility, people will pay almost anything for your work.

Obtain a medal. (Note that medals with five-pointed stars, crosses, or crowns hold a great deal of magical power.) These are easily found in secondhand stores or flea markets. Even better if you have your own or one passed down through your family. Write your name on a piece of yellow silk. Sprinkle cinnamon powder and a crushed bay leaf in the silk and wrap the medal up in the piece of silk. Yellow is the color of recognition and glory. Silk is used by witches to enhance the power of a talisman. Cinnamon is sacred to Chango, the god who rules *iwa pele*; good character. Laurel was used by the ancient Greeks to crown victors in the Pythian games and bay is a species of laurel. It became associated with all forms of success and winning. Carry this talisman or keep around the workplace to help you gain respect, honor, recognition, and advancement in your field.

BANISH FEAR OF SUCCESS

INGREDIENTS

aloe leaf
paprika
ginger root
tumeric

These ingredients should be sewn into a black silk cloth using red and orange thread. Carry the pouch with you to overcome your fear of success.

Aloe is said to soothe fears and phobias. Paprika is for love and courage. Ginger root promotes fearlessness. Tumeric is a purifying agent and drives out all obstacles. The combination should relax you, help you overcome worry, and then push you out over the edge so that you can fly toward your success. The color black is used to absorb fear and negativity. Red represents action and energy. Orange opens channels and is the color of success.

BEAN MAGIC

INGREDIENTS
assorted dried beans

In ancient Greece and Rome, beans were held in such high esteem that they were employed to count votes. White beans signified a yes vote while black beans signified a no vote. The bean-count system was very clear and precise. Official documents record no terms such as *chad* or *hanging chad* to characterize discrepancies within their bean-poll ballots.[1] However there was some talk on the ancient astral grapevine concerning an inaccurate bean count that occurred in West Palmyra in A.D. 272. The citizens of Palmyra were asked to vote on whether or not they wanted Queen Zenobia to continue to rule in proxy for her infant son. Since the murder of her husband, Septimius Odenathus, Zenobia had been doing an excellent job ruling Palmyra. She had decreased the national debt and unemployment rate and expanded the territories all the way into Egypt. Her ambition caught the watchful eye of Rome. It is rumored that during this vote, an official from the party of the republic of Rome surreptitiously placed a large sack of *lividus faba* or *mávromatika* outside a voting booth in the western district. Voters in that area mistakenly drew from this sack and at the tallying over

---

[1]An official Chad did not appear until the early 1900s when the French colonized parts of the African continent!

ten thousand votes had to be disqualified because they were essentially cast with black-eyed peas. There was no way to determine whether the voters meant a white bean to signify yes or a black bean to signify no. The bureaucrats and lawyers of West Palmyra fought for months over the ballots, counting and recounting, and in the meantime Aurelian sent an army to usurp Zenobia from the throne and led her captive back to Rome. She spent her last years living on a welfare check doled out by the Roman Empire while her beautiful Palmyra fell into ruin. After this tragic episode it was decided to replace the bean count with the paper ballot and/or assassination attempts in order to elect new heads of state.

Beans are still used to make personal decisions. I know one top executive who keeps a bowl of black and white dried beans on his desk. He often reaches in to grab a handful and then takes a count. If he has pulled mostly white beans, the answer is yes. Mostly black beans, the answer is no. Equal amounts, he waits another day and asks again. Apparently people have been hired or fired, stocks bought or sold based solely on the number of black or white beans that lay in the palm of his hand. This man is no King Solomon (although it is important to note that he is rich and successful) and he does not use the beans for rational decision making. He uses them when he needs to get in touch with his intuition. When logical thinking cannot assist him in making the right choice. The procedure is much like flipping a coin, and calling heads or tails to exact an answer. However according to various mythologies and lore, beans, unlike coins, are said to talk. They speak to humans and give them magical counsel. It is widely believed that wise spirits dwell in beans and they can be called upon for advice and direction. Because many beans have "eyes" they are said to bring vision. I suggest you try this method when your head and heart hold no clue.

But there's more to beans than black and white. Beans come in a myriad of colors, sizes, and shapes. There are one hundred and fifty species and countless varieties of beans. Beans are believed to make wishes come true. Beans are representative of the internal organs and of the brain. They can be used for healing. They are also used in money magic because they represent the richness of the harvest crop. The assortment of colors represent the numerous paths of success: intellectual, psychological, material, emotional, and spiritual.

The following is a guide to specific beans and their magical associations:

black turtles—help in jumping hurdles, decision making, protection, concentration
butter beans—stress reduction, removal of obstacles
canary beans—success in the arts, happiness, communication
cranberry (October) beans—opportunity, attraction
fava beans—power
field (cow) peas/black-eyed—luck, vision
garbanzo (chickpea)—strength in battle and competition
great northern—discovery, spirituality, insight, guards plans
green baby lima—new sources of income
green splits—money, health
green pigeon—money, resourcefulness

large lima—financial growth and expansion
lentils—peace, tranquility, financial security
navy beans—strength, determination
oval white beans—opportunity, protection of assets
pinto beans—action, movement, opens channels
roman beans—power, conquest, precision
pinks—confidence, romance
red kidney—wisdom, foresight, love, healing
small reds—energy, lust
speckled lima—networking
whole green beans—money
yellow splits—luck, creativity, fame

My personal method of magic is to keep a jar of as-sorted colored dried beans on my altar at all times. They keep the lines of communication, creativity, and prosperity open. I like to run both my hands through the beans for inspiration. The beans do not need to be replaced until a full lunar year (thirteen full moons), although it is advis-able to make sure the beans are clean and dust free on every new moon. Check for cracked or flaked shells. Dis-pose of and replace these. I also like to hold specific beans under my tongue while making my wishes. I find that the spirit within the bean can speak more clearly to me when I hold it under the tongue. However when I am unclear as to what it is I am wishing for, beans held in the left hand seem to result in surprising events that cheer me up greatly. On full moons, I part with some of my precious beans and sprinkle them outdoors (in the four directions) as offerings of gratitude to the divine ones.

All beans are ruled by Mercury, the god/planet of creativity, messages, and communication. They are a wonderful talisman for writers, educators, or those in creative fields who need to communicate and teach ideas. Mercury is also known as the trickster. It is said that the stripes on the bean came to be because the beans laughed so hard their sides split. Comedians should eat[2] or carry speckled beans to improve their sense of humor and wit. The wing-footed Mercury was quick to snatch the bean up as his own. Yet it seems that many gods favor beans. The Maya, Aztecs, Greeks, Romans, Egyptians, Japanese, and Chinese all offered beans to their gods and goddesses. Ramses III once presented over eleven thousand jars of beans to the gods in one offering.

Beans were sacrificed to Apollo. If you are an actor or in the arts, give Apollo an offering of beans. Sprinkle them outside under a rising sun and ask Apollo to grant your career requests. Beans are also pole climbers. They like to ascend to the top. They are wonderful magical and psychological aids for those who feel lost in their path or those who feel they have made foolish mistakes that cannot be undone. The bean will lead you up and out of misfortune and ruin.[3] The bean can also help those who are clear about their paths to ascend higher and more quickly up the ladder of success.[4] If you are seeking direction or promotion, soak in a tub of assorted beans on a new moon

---

[2]Soak beans overnight. Drain, rinse and submerge in fresh water before cooking to counteract the effects of gas.

[3]Butter, great northern, and pinks are best for this use.

[4]Black turtles, fava, and whole green are the ideal choice here.

to magnetize your aura and increase your wealth and position.

In some cultures beans were so sacred they could not be touched, eaten, or even spoken of out loud. They were given as offerings to appease and feed the spirits of the dead. Funeral directors, morticians, medical examiners, and hired hit men should all refrain from eating beans but rather quietly sprinkle them around the workplace while wearing surgical gloves. Beans like to link the living with the dead and can be used by anyone who needs to obtain the advice or power of a deceased person. The bean is a great tool for the actor to get in touch with a historical character he or she is portraying, and is the ultimate tool for the historian or clairvoyant to look accurately into the past. In 2 Samuel, beans are mentioned as one of the foods eaten by King David's army to renew their strength for battle. Beans can be eaten by soldiers for victory and success in combat.

The most famous bean fable is that of Jack and the Beanstalk. Jack traded the family cow for a sack of worthless beans. When his mother tossed them out the window a huge beanstalk grew. Jack climbed the stalk all the way to a giant's castle in the sky. He escaped being eaten by the ogre and stole all his treasures while the giant slept. Finally Jack cut down the stalk, and sent the nasty giant toppling to his death. Do you have a huge competitor, an ogre of a boss, or a large corporation trying to fee-fi-fo-fum you into ruin? Plant a jack bean and when it climbs to the top of the pole, cut it down calling out the name of the fee-fi-foe you would like to slay. It is also believed that the purple-and-white flowers of the jack bean can bring legal success. If you are suing a large corporation carry the flowers in your pocket when you go to court.

Remember that beans are very sacred and carry a high spiritual vibration. Do not try to cheat your way to the top while using bean magic. The bean is the talisman of the magical hero/heroine whom the gods favor.

BEAT OUT COMPETITION

INGREDIENTS

skin of a mango

The skin of a mango is used in protection rituals. Belonging to the poison ivy and poison sumac family, the sap inside the skin of the fruit can cause severe allergic reactions to many people. If you are allergic to mangoes, this is not the spell for you.

Carve your name or the name of your business inside a piece of the fresh skin of a mango. Let the skin dry out and then place in a cloth teabag as a talisman against harmful competition. You can carry the bag or hide it in your office. No one will be able to touch you or your business as a result.

BIG FAT F'ING LOSER SPELL

INGREDIENTS

head of broccoli
chervil, chickweed, or cilantro

This is the point where you readers will think, and even say out loud: "Now I know this witch has lost her marbles. Who in his or her right mind is going to want to perform a spell to become a big fat f'ing loser?!!" Well, here's where you are mistaken. The Big Fat F'ing Loser spell can come in very handy. In fact the more successful you are, the more necessary this spell may become.

My friend T and I use it all the time. Basically your choices narrow down to this. Use the Big Fat F'ing Loser spell or constantly make up lies about what you do for a living and eventually Get Caught in them.

You see, before T and I began to perform the Big Fat F'ing Loser spell, we could never have a good relaxing time when we went out. People would ask what we did for a living and once we told them, they attached themselves to us all night. T and I never got a chance to dance or drink together or boast and brag about who had the bigger green thumb. I was busy all night giving my psychic impressions to strangers, or telling them how to get a book published, or trying to worm my way out of reading and rewriting their manuscripts. T, who is a big casting agent, had strangers auditioning for him all night. This became very stressful

as we are mostly polite people. So instead of relaxing, playing, and blowing off steam, we were really working over-
time.

One night, we decided to lie about our jobs. I said that
I freelanced passing out flyers for different delis and fast-
food chains. Or that I worked in the returns department of
a large retail store (but I only did this the month after
Christmas. The rest of the year I sold my blood and got
paid to be a guinea pig for experimental pharmaceuticals).
T told most people he was an unemployed busboy. But
particularly annoying people were told that he took mea-
surements for colostomy bags and emptied containers of
cellulite for a plastic surgeon. Honestly, these people wanted
nothing to do with us! Eventually these lies caught up with
us because we'd forgotten all the stories we told. And when
people somehow found out the truth, then they thought we
were big f'ing lying a'holes. We don't want to come off as
big f'ing lying a'holes, but the idea of putting on the big
fat f'ing loser mask greatly appealed to us. Since performing
this spell, people rarely even ask us what we do. They just
assume that we are big fat f'ing losers and have nothing to
offer. They leave us alone. T and I are free to have our big
fat f'ing loser fun.

Now, if you have a big enough ego to perform this spell,
this is how it goes. Take a big fat head of broccoli. Broccoli
is considered the biggest loser of the vegetable world. Even
though it is reported to deter the growth of cancer cells and
has wonderful protective properties, it is often either
shunned or ignored (especially by stupid people). Steam,
season the broccoli with chervil, and eat, or add to bath-

water. Chervil is not very easy to find. Almost no one even knows what chervil is or what chervil does for a living. Most people don't even care. This makes it perfect for the spell. If you cannot obtain chervil try using chickweed. Chickweed is alleged to make you appear smaller than you really are. If you can't find chickweed, substitute cilantro. Cilantro is used to guard against evil and intrusion and can be used to protect or conceal identities. If you can't find cilantro, you really are a big fat f'ing loser and I don't think you need this spell. Try The Minute You Walked into the Room spell instead.

BIG FAT F'ING LOSER SPELL II OR, THE REMOVAL OF DIFFICULT CURSES SPELL

So you're no King Midas. Everything *you* touch turns to sh——! Nothing you do turns out right. You're a big f'ing loser, and not only that, you're cursed. You must be cursed. You were cursed before you were even born. Your whole family was cursed. It's never your fault when something goes wrong, it's those unlucky stars you were born under and that ancient family curse. Yes, I've seen you before. I know who you are. You have three choices to remedy your situation.

Choice #1: Stop blaming the universe and take responsibility for your life.

Choice #2: Find a pseudogypsy who will remove your

curse by "burying" $10,000 of your hard-earned cash in the "cemetery."[1]

Choice #3: Do one of the following spells.

I. If you truly are cursed, especially if it is a family curse, you *are* supposed to bury something in the cemetery. But it is *not* your hard-earned cash for someone else to dig up later. Nope, only a real loser would fall for something like that. First of all, spells using money to lift curses or alleviate sin *have to be given to charity* in order for the spell to be effective. And this is a fine way to remove financial blocks. Give some of the green away. But know who you are giving it to and be sure that you think it is a worthy cause.

What should be buried in the cemetery is a broken mirror[2] or a footprint. Yes, that's right—a footprint. To remove the very worst kind of curse, leave a trail of footprints through a cemetery and then wipe them out. This is believed to kill off the trail of bad luck or any curse that may have been following you. Now, how is it possible to walk through a cemetery and get out without leaving foot prints? Well, it can be done. Enter and carefully walk nine paces in. Then walk backward, bending over and brushing away or "burying" your footprints as you go, up until your very last step through the cemetery gate.[3] You must chant the following verse nine times:

---

[1] In pseudogypsy language the word *burying* is translated as "hiding," "stashing," or "depositing." The word *cemetery* can mean "under my pseudogypsy bed" or "in my pseudogypsy bank account, you sucker!"

[2] But *only* if you have accidentally broken one, because this can cause very bad luck!

[3] Many cemeteries do not have gates, but those that do are said to be the most magical.

Here at the gates of death I stand.
Undo this curse by my command.
Go! Vanish as the print of shoe.
Let me begin my path anew.

It is said that using a peacock feather to dust away the prints will bring extremely good luck and add potency to the spell. The sighting of a live peacock in a cemetery is said to wipe out even the strongest, longest, biggest, baddest, darkest of curses. The peacock is the sign of the goddess in her most merciful and benevolent aspect.

II. There is another method of performing this spell, but I suggest you stick with the first unless you are desperate enough to part with your most favorite pair of shoes (the ones you walk in the most). Shoes represent the path we walk in life and it is possible to change our path (or our luck) by changing our shoes.[4] There are also many superstitions about wearing the shoes of a dead person. It is very bad luck. I therefore advise you not to buy used shoes, as you do not know where they have come from. If you feel you are walking a cursed path, an easy way to break the curse is to leave a pair of your shoes at the gates of a cemetery. Chant the following verse nine times:

Here at the gates of death I stand.
Undo this curse by my command.

---

[4] Shoes may also represent the vagina, and can be used for sex magic, but that is for another book. Stay tuned, dear reader!

> *I leave the curse within this shoe*
> *as I begin my path anew.*

Put on a new pair of shoes and walk away without looking back. It is also said that the dead need shoes for their journey through the underworld. If you feel you need the assistance of some spirits on the other side to break your curse, leaving a pair of shoes is a good way to win the spirits' favor. It is also good if you feel your curse is caused by a spirit that is haunting you. In this case leave a new pair of shoes, so the spirit of the dead person can put them on, get going on his or her new path, and leave you alone. High heels are also reccomended to elevate spirits to the heavenly realms.

III. This third spell is for those readers who prefer to remove their curses in the comfort of their own homes. These readers may be cursed but they are certainly not *crazy!* And right now they are thinking *No way in hell my 'barking dogs' are going to part with their Hush Puppies!* or *Cemeteries give me the willies. Only* real *losers hang out in the graveyard. No, no, that's not for me!*

Okay, I've got you covered. You must eat three eggs on a new moon and crush and burn and completely destroy the shells. Chant this nine times as the shells are burning:

> *Eat the egg burn the shell.*
> *I command and compel*
> *with this magical verse*
> *to be free of this curse.*

The eating of the egg on the new moon is symbolic of rebirth. The destruction of the shell symbolizes removing any trace of your origin. It is used to destroy any link between yourself and the curse. This spell is very effective when the magic used against you involved some form of sympathetic link, for example, your hair or signature or clothing, etc. was used by someone to place a curse on you. Bury the burnt remains of eggshell in the ground or toss them to the wind or into a body of running water. (A running faucet or flush toilet will suffice.)

Feel confident in performing your ritual. It will work. There is no curse that cannot be lifted. Well, except—a mother's curse. They say this is the most powerful curse of all. There is no remedy. It cannot be lifted. I can only advise you to take preventative measures against the mothers' curse.

1. Be good to your mother. Do not incur her wrath.
2. Do not murder the children of any mother. If you have already done so, make sure this woman never looks you in the eye. Otherwise you will be eternally damned!

BREATH FOR SUCCESS

INGREDIENTS
assorted breath fresheners

We generally think of sweetening or freshening our breath for a lover in preparation for a kiss. But unless your job puts you in front of a computer at all times, unless you have absolutely no human contact at work, bad breath can be the kiss of death in business. Here are some guidelines on the properties of the most common gums, candies, mints, and breath fresheners on the market. I will begin with the herbs.

Peppermint brings energy and also has sex appeal. This may or may not be appropriate on the job. However mint and cherry combined tone down the seductive element of the mint and summon positive, vibrant rays of magnetism and self-confidence. Spearmint is used for knowledge and memory. It's very good to use when you have to make a presentation, and is recommended for teachers or students. Wintergreen is used to break obstacles, for protection, and also to attract friendly nature spirits of luck and good fortune.

The second group are aromatic spices. Cloves can be sucked or chewed for business expansion and/or protection of wealth. They are ruled by Jupiter. I recommend clove for investors. Cardamom and clove are best for politicians, salespeople, and gigolos. Cardamom brings eloquence to the tongue and clove will assist in attracting money. Cardamom alone is best for anyone who does public speaking or presentation, and cardamom is also used to woo. Add clove when you are trying to win over people's money. Anise or licorice have many wonderful properties. The first is Neptunian and creative. If you are an artist, designer, or filmmaker use this to freshen the breath. Anise also draws money, and it is believed to make one youthful in appearance. I recommend chewing anise seed or licorice before a job interview. It will help you speak creatively, look younger, and draw the salary you hope for.

Last, but not least, the fruits and a flower. Lemon candies provide soothing calm energy. Best to suck on before trouble-shooting. Lemon also cleanses and removes obstacles. Cherry has been mentioned. Orange is good for forming partnerships. Lime is great for personal power and a commanding presence. Cinnamon is an all-around good-luck-and-blessing formula and it also brings positive changes speedily. It can be used when you have to act quickly. Violet used in the spring makes wishes come true. It is used year round for protection and to change one's fortune.

CATCH A RICH HUSBAND

INGREDIENTS

jasmine rice
orange flower water
saffron
almonds
golden raisins
green tomato
Hungarian paprika

Wedding a rich man absolutely falls under the category of a professional pursuit. It is a serious career. And if you don't think so, you are kidding yourself and will probably not be successful at it. There are too many women (and men) working full-time to achieve this goal. The competition is stiff. You are going to need some powerful magical assistance, and here is what I propose: Beginning on the first Friday following the new moon, prepare and eat jasmine rice seasoned with orange flower water, saffron, almonds, and golden raisins. Prepare and eat again on all Fridays up until 2 days after the full moon. Repeat for three more lunar cycles, then do not repeat for one year. Jasmine, rice, and orange flower are all used to bring love and proposals of marriage. Saffron, almonds, and golden raisins are eaten to obtain great fortune and wealth.

If you know which rich man you want to wed, carve both your names on the skin of a green tomato. Green tomatoes symbolize both money and love. Roll the tomato in Hungarian paprika to force a proposal of marriage. Do this spell on a Friday during a waxing moon and present this as an offering to the river goddess Oshun. She rules both love and money matters. As you throw the paprika tomato into the river tell Oshun what you want. Promise her five golden coins or five golden rings dipped in honey when she fulfills your request. Oshun usually does not deliver unless she is rewarded before and afterward. Do not forget those honey-dipped coins or rings, or Oshun may see to it that your marriage is dissolved. Even worse, dissolved without alimony!

CHANGE CAREERS

INGREDIENTS

pimiento
pine nuts
eggplant (optional)

These ingredients are ruled by Scorpio, the astrological sign of death and rebirth. They are wonderful foods to eat when you need the spiritual strength to let go and make a change. Pine nuts were eaten by the Romans to attract money and strength. Pimientos give courage, ambition, and add fuel to the creative fires. If you are in a dead-end job or career but afraid to let go and make a change, supplement your daily diet with pine nuts and pimiento. If you are confused about career direction, add eggplant to inspire you with a new plan.

CONNECTION SPELL

INGREDIENTS

lavender flowers
cinnamon powder
marjoram

The number you are dialing is busy. Finally you get through only to be put on hold indefinitely. You go on-line. After an endless search you find what you are looking for, only to be bumped off-line before you can download the information. How much time, energy, and money do you waste because of these annoying occurrences? If your business depends on phone lines or Internet service, you need a spell to improve your connections. Even if you are out of work and collecting unemployment, sometimes it feels as though you could become a millionaire in all the time it takes you to get through the bureaucratic red tape! In any situation in which you need to improve the lines of communication, simply hold some lavender flowers and cinnamon powder in the palm of the right hand or place a dish of lavender and cinnamon powder near the phone or computer. These mercurial herbs will help the lines of communication to open up and run more smoothly. I have used them countless times with quick and positive results, even during a dreaded Mercury retrograde.

By adding a third ingredient you can attract clients to call you or to hit your Web site. Marjoram is another mercurial spice that is believed to guarantee money. Added to cinnamon and lavender it will open the lines of communication to increase income. Hold in the palm of the right hand and visualize business coming in, or place them in a bowl next to your phone or computer modem. These three ingredients can also be added to the bathwater for those who need to communicate or pitch ideas for financial backing. Take a magical bath the night before or morning of your business meeting. Soak in the tub for at least ten minutes and burn orange and green candles next to the tub while you bathe.

EDUCATION SPELL

INGREDIENTS

lavender
cinnamon
pink roses
sage
olives or olive oil

This spell is for both teachers and students. It is designed to increase the capacity to absorb knowledge and information and also to bring success in the field of study and education.

Lavender and cinnamon are sacred to Hermes, the ruler of Gemini, which is the sign of communication and education. Lavender and cinnamon improve study habits and open the mind to receive knowledge. Pink roses are associated with wisdom and perception. Sage is sacred to Sagittarius and higher learning. Pink roses and sage transform knowledge into wisdom and also alleviate stress. Olives or olive oil bring success and recognition in the field of education. They are sacred to Athena, the goddess of intelligence.

Keep a bowl of lavender flowers, cinnamon sticks, pink roses (dried or fresh), and sage (fresh or dried) in the room where you study or teach. You can also carry sachets in the pocket. Work olives or olive oil into your diet especially on new and full moons to give you stamina in your quest for knowledge and to bring you continued success and recognition.

FLAPJACKS FOR SUCCESS

INGREDIENTS

pancake mix
butter
fruit (optional)
maple syrup

The pancake or flapjack originated in 2600 B.C. in Egypt. By A.D. 461 the pancake became associated with shriving or the atonement of sins. Mardi Gras or Fat Tuesday eventually became known as Pancake Day. Pancakes were eaten before the onset of Lent to symbolically summon rebirth (egg), innocence (milk), and staples of life (flour). Legend has it that a British woman in the fifteenth century was in such a hurry to attend church when she heard the church bell that she ran to the church with her frying pan and flapjacks still in hand. Thus began the British tradition of the annual flapjack race to church. It is still practiced to this day. Women must be over eighteen years of age. They run a distance of four hundred and fifteen yards and must "flap jacks" at least three times during the race.

So in modern times, flapping and eating pancakes has also come to symbolically represent success in races or competition, particularly where women are concerned. The ritual of flapping jacks and then eating them can be done not only once a year but on every or any new moon. Use the ritual to summon renewal and cleansing and to clear your path of any career obstacles. Also use the ritual to bring you success in winning or any professional situation where you need to beat out competition. You need not run to church with your frying pan, for the Goddess traditionally abides in every hearth (or kitchen).

Grease your pan with butter and visualize your own path being as smooth as butter. You might also want to visualize any person who needs buttering up in order for you to succeed. Add fruit slices to pan. Blueberry for protection, cherry for self-confidence, banana for networking, straw-berry to gain admiration. Pour in batter and flip when edges are brown. As you flip (or flap) call your wishes for success out loud. Make sure to flip the cakes at least three times.

Three is the magical number of the Goddess and also represents completion.

Another magical association. In the tarot, the jack of fire (or wands) is the card of career advancement or promotion. Flapping jacks over a fire (gas, not electric) also promotes change and upwardly mobile movement. To seal in the magic, anoint flapjacks with maple syrup to make your wishes stick to you. Eat and record all results that take place within the next fourteen days (the full moon). This spell is most effective when done in stages. Make your goals clear and in steps. On the following new moon, repeat the process with further goals. Best results occur when performed for three new moons in a row.

FOR LUCK AT THE RACETRACK

INGREDIENTS

a horseshoe
root beer or sarsaparilla
cornmeal and/or buckwheat
goblet of pewter or silver
wheat-back pennies

You will need an altar or small table to perform this spell. Lay all your betting forms or any paperwork having to do with your horses underneath the table or altar. Place a horseshoe on top of the altar. The open arc of the horseshoe should be facing away from you as you look at it. Place a goblet of pewter or silver in the center of the horseshoe. Fill the goblet with sarsaparilla or root beer. Sprinkle buckwheat and/or cornmeal in a circle around the goblet. Drop wheat-back pennies into the goblet until the liquid overflows onto the circle of cornmeal and/or buckwheat. Dip your index fingers into this mixture. Rub your pockets with your index fingers. Dip your fingers again and lightly touch the outer corners of your eyes. Dip a third time and rub your hands vigorously together. Now gather and touch all documents placed under the table. Repeat before choosing all bets or before all races in which your horse will compete.

In kabalistic magic, an overflowing cup signifies great wealth and luck. To anoint one's pockets with liquid overflowing from the cup brings money. To anoint the eyes brings vision and intuition. It is believed that luck and success will come to the first thing that is touched by the hands that were anointed with this mixture. Epona is the goddess of horses. Her magical symbols include the horseshoe, the goblet, corn and grain. Corn is used in prosperity spells. Buckwheat is a grain sacred not only to Epona but to Jupiter as well. Jupiter is the ruler of Sagittarius, the astrological sign of the horse. Buckwheat is used for financial expansion. Sarsaparilla is ruled by Sagittarius and is used to draw money. Using wheat-back pennies adds the element of luck. Pennies along with horseshoes have a long magical history associated with luck. The metals silver and pewter are associated with speed.

Another powerful symbol of Epona is the cornucopia. This spell can also be prepared in dry form. Place all your documents on the altar. Put the horseshoe on top of them. Place the goblet in the center of the horseshoe. Fill the goblet with dried sarsaparilla, cornmeal, buckwheat, and wheat-back pennies. Tip the goblet over on its side as if it were a cornucopia. Allow some of the grain, herb, and coins to spill onto your paperwork. Good luck at the races!

FRESH START SPELL

INGREDIENTS

sea salt
lemon
fresh dill
fresh carrots, corn, beets, snow peas
fresh tuna steak
fresh ground pepper
fresh olive oil
romaine lettuce

I. A magical bath should be taken on or near a new moon just as you are about to look for a new job or begin a new venture. The bath is essentially used to cleanse and remove obstacles in your new path or direction. Other ingredients work to open positive channels and generate prosperity. This bath is especially useful for those who have changed jobs frequently in the past few years and are tired of making lateral moves. It is also beneficial to the person who has had difficulty finding any employment and it is designed as well for those needing a fresh start because they are making a career change.

Begin by filling a tub with warm water and adding the juice of a whole lemon. Add three fistfuls of salt and three sprigs of fresh dill. Boil some unpeeled beets and add this water to the bath. Add some carrot tops and corn silk from freshly shucked corn. You must also add three snow peas to the bath. Snow peas are available year-round.

It is important that all ingredients be fresh for this spell. This means that its performance may be limited to a specific time of the year, the fall or harvest period. Generally my advice is to use whatever you can get your hands on: fresh, frozen, or canned. But with this particular spell, the effectiveness will be based on the freshness of the ingredients. Please refer to other spells of a similar nature if you are unable to obtain these ingredients.

Salt and lemon are purifiers and path openers. Salt also represents grounding, sustenance, and prosperity. Dill is sacred to Mercury and is used for opening channels, both creative and financial. Beets are ruled by Saturn and are used in the search for employment. Carrots lend vision, energy, and ambition. Corn is complex and varied in its energy, emitting a high spiritual vibration as well as one of material well-being. Corn silk is used to uncover hidden wealth or potential. The pea is associated with the planet Venus or the sign of Libra. It is a mediator, bringing balance and peace into the life. After adding all ingredients to the tub, soak for a minimum of ten minutes and visualize your new career path opening before you.

II. On the full moon (approximately fourteen days after the new moon) the second part of this spell should be performed. I find that working the same magic from a new to full-moon period brings the best results. On the full moon obtain a fresh tuna steak. Carve your name or initials into the tuna. Tuna is a symbol of prosperity and protection. Add some fresh pepper and fresh olive oil to a pan. Heat and sear the tuna. Pepper deters enemies or competition and olive oil brings long-lasting prosperity. Searing is an action that will help you to magically cut or burn your path clearly into existence. Add three pinches of salt to lessen anxiety, remove negativity, and draw money. A dash of lemon juice and pinch of dill will cleanse and season with success.

After the tuna is cooked, place it on a plate of romaine lettuce. Dark leafy lettuce is used to invoke strong and continual prosperity. Garnish the plate with fresh carrots, corn, beets, and peas. Meditate on all your goals, hopes, and professional dreams for ten minutes in front of this plate. At this time the food should be eaten to infuse you with all this wonderful magic. However, if you dislike or have allergies to any of these ingredients, do not consume. Simply leave the plate out on a table or altar as an offering. Meditate upon it continually for another day as you would meditate upon a burning candle. On the evening following the full moon, you may dispose of this plate of food. Say thank you before doing so. Allow at least another new moon cycle to pass in order to see the positive effects of this spell.

HANDSHAKE MAGIC

INGREDIENTS

I.

pure lanolin

II.

salt

I. The hand is a symbol of power, protection, divinity, luck, and good fortune. A whole life can be seen in the lines of the hand. Superstitions and fears abound regarding the shaking of hands. One New York real estate mogul refuses to shake hands. This is because he imagines some fellow has just come from the bathroom without washing his hands. The mogul is loath to shake this hand that has been you know where, while he is buttering his bread.

Aside from the obvious phobia of contamination, this tycoon's deeper instincts are actually correct. It is believed that magical power can be stolen through the hands. In some cultures, the hands are considered more intimate than the genitals. The touching of hands signifies the transference of divine power to mortals. Michelangelo depicted this on the ceiling of the Sistine Chapel with the finger of G-d reaching out toward the finger of Adam (mankind). The ancient Babylonian and Egyptian rites of kingship involved shaking hands with the statue of a god to receive the power of rulership. The Egyptian hieroglyph of an outstretched hand means "to give." It was an intimate rite reserved and practiced only between gods and kings. Handshaking taboos still exist in the 21st century. There is a practice among spiritualists to reach farther down and grasp the wrist of the person whose hand is being shaken instead of his or her palm. This method evolved from the ancient belief that the touching or rubbing of palms together could cause people to exchange fates. There is another handshaking practice commonly used by politicians (whether they employ this method consciously or unconsciously, I do not know). They often shake with both hands. When the right hand is extended to grasp the right hand of another, the left hand is then used to cover both right hands. By cupping the hand of another between your own hands and allowing the fingers of your left and right hand to meet, you create a circle of energy that allows your power to flow back through your left hand and not escape you. The Japanese custom of greeting, the clasping of one's own hands together with a slight bow of the head is considered a safer and more civilized form of greeting and acknowledgment. The modern or alternate European custom of kissing both cheeks is also less intrusive. However it is often necessary to extend the hand in business and social situations in order not to appear off-putting. If you find it problematic to shake hands, or experience a loss or draining of energy after doing so, you should rub pure lanolin into the hands to seal and protect your aura.

II. In medieval times, men meeting upon the road might pull out their weapons to fight. After deciding not to fight, the knives were dropped and the right hand was extended (the weapon hand) as a symbol of peace/truce. In business it is customary to shake hands upon meeting and also after agreeing on deals. A handshake is used as an affirmation of one's word (although it is always best to get something in writing). In this sense the handshake is your signature and the calling card of your reputation. You may want to focus on projecting an image out through the hands in addition to safeguarding and locking in your power. There is a long magical history and tradition of dusting the hands with various potions to create numerous effects. Salt is used for purification and protection. It is very useful in overcoming obstacles in negotiations. It builds confidence, promotes success, and draws money.

Rub a pinch of salt vigorously between the palms (do not do this if you have any open cuts on your hands) to project your power without the risk of losing it. I recommend using Argentine salt if you can find it. Argentines have more self-confidence than any other peoples in the world. A second-best choice would be French salt. Third-best choices are coarse salt, sea salt, or kosher salt. Using salt indigenous to the area you are working in is also favored. This ritual should be done in the morning before you begin your day, or you could keep some salt handy in the office and use just before business meetings. It is very important that you be alone while performing this ritual. Performing it in front of others will weaken its power.

HOW TO DEAL WITH SNOTTY SALESPEOPLE

INGREDIENTS

bee pollen
grated orange peel
saffron

One of the most annoying things is having salespeople be rude to us as we drop money into their establishments. How many times has your day been ruined by a nasty cab driver, waiter, sales clerk, phone operator, car mechanic, bank teller or some other impudent, surly service person?

This is a great powder to sprinkle around yourself before a day of shopping (especially if you are headed for the returns department), or any day that involves heavy-duty interaction with sales or service people. I call it the Queen Bee formula. It is designed to give you an air of importance and rulership and to put all the little drones in their rightful place, which happens to be waiting on you hand and foot. Use this formula to get fast, efficient, courteous service with a smile.

Sprinkle bee pollen, orange peel, and saffron in a majestic path before yourself. Do this as if you were rolling out a red carpet. Walk across the mixture in bare feet, then put your shoes on, go out, and have a wonderful day. These three ingredients are sacred to the Goddess in her most powerful yet loving aspect. They will invoke a kind of subconscious devotion and dedication from others. They will treat you as though you were the Great Mother Herself. By the way, if this potion is placed under the tongue before kissing someone, it will make the one receiving the kiss devoted and loyal to you alone.

JOB PROTECTION SPELL

INGREDIENTS

mixed-berry yogurt
fresh green salad*
red and/or white radish
salt
olive oil
fresh lemon juice

I have often encountered people coming in for magical advice because they feel their jobs are being threatened. The question most frequently asked of my tarot cards in the past twenty years has not been "Does s/he love me?" but rather "Am I going to lose my job?" This potion is designed to protect your position. (See To Regain a Position spell if you have already been canned.)

Yogurt is ruled by the nurturing Mother Goddess. It represents and draws forth spiritual, emotional, and material sustenance. Berries are used for magical protection. It is also believed that berries ward off envy or jealousy. Berries can

---

*A combination of dark greens: lettuce (not iceberg), or spinach, arugula, beet tops, cilantro, parsley, watercress, and basil are all good choices.

also be used to arrest negative competition. I suggest eating mixed-berry yogurt for breakfast every third day for at least a full lunar cycle (that's twenty-eight days from new moon to new moon).

A green salad including red or white radishes should be added to the lunch or dinner menu every third day for half a lunar cycle (new moon to full moon). Greens draw money, prosperity, security. In combination with radish you are creating a protective shield around your source of income. Prepare the greens in the center of the plate. Add a pinch of salt, olive oil, and lemon. All three dressing ingredients are for protection and purification. Salt and olive oil also enhance prosperity. Slice the radishes and arrange them in a circle around the perimeter of the plate to form a circle around the greens. Remember, in magic presentation counts for a lot. The plate is in essence your altar. Use a green or blue or white plate for best results. Before eating, visualize your job and your income being protected, surrounded by a circle of white light. Begin by eating some greens and then eat a few radish slices every other bite. This spell is most effective when performed (eaten) on the job site.

LAS GUERRERAS/ THE WARRIORS

La Guerrera does not live in a man's world. She lives in a warrior's world. Men are merely her prey. She likes to catch them off guard, to tempt them, to taunt them, to squeeze their hearts until their wallets and bank accounts and credit cards and hot tips on the racetrack and stock portfolios come tumbling out and fall at her feet. La Guerrera is a different breed than el Gato (the Cat). El Gato is a fine seducer, but she is hardly as furrocious. She is a purring pussycat easily satisfied by a man paying her way. La Guerrera is much more complicated and not as easily satisfied. She wants everything men have. For her own. La Guerrera puts out nothing in exchange, unlike the "puts-out" pussy. El Gato will only show her claws after the goods have been delivered, la Guerrera has all her tools sharpened from the top. She carries an atomic arsenal beneath her skirt. All men fall in love with her, but la Guerrera isn't looking for love. That is not to say that the Warrior does not enjoy pleasure. She takes her pleasure when and where and with whom she pleases. What she's looking for is a strategic way in. She wants to be on top. She wants to rule the world. In order to do that, she must first bring the world reeling to its knees. Not only is the Warrior a witch, she's a downright bitch! Don't get me wrong. I love the Warriors. I love to watch them in action.

I have seen the military and tactical magic of las Guerreras. It is very intense and powerful. Being trained in the sacred art of invisibility, I have been able to observe them closely and can now report their top-secret rituals. I have seen them at dusk just as the light of day begins to fade. At the onset of moonrise is when they start their work. When the light of the Goddess overpowers the light of the Sun God. I have seen how they begin their vampiric day. They don't eat much. They are lean and hungry like Cassius. Upon rising they gargle with a potion of rum and chili pepper juice. They spit this out seven times while calling out the names of those they will hunt down. Then they chew on very potent mint leaves to cover up the scent of war. Rum is sacred to Chango and chili is sacred to Mars, two warrior gods. Mint is the lusty herb of the underworld. This makes them sexy, powerful, and in control. They listen to tuba tango and marching bands. "Persian March" by Strauss is a favorite tune, along with the Triumphal Procession in Verdi's *Aida*. They play it over and over as they meticulously grind whole black peppercorns to add to their warrior red lipstick and combat crimson nail polish. And with these red-and-black-flecked mixtures, they paint their poised lips and the toenails that will complement the open-toe fronts of their rapier-heeled shoes. The spiked heels are also magically anointed for power and conquest by being plunged into limes. The Warriors do different things. I cannot report upon it all. She knows that it is her looks, her ways that win her fortune and inside information. She uses this to the utmost. The preparation is elaborate. Every item, every asset is enchanted and bewitched. A lipstick is never just a lipstick, nor a stocking, nor a shoe. Her eyeliner is loaded. She's got ammunition up the wazoo.

I saw one of them draw a bath. She sat naked with a pair of nail clippers on the edge of the tub. Before her sat a huge bouquet of roses—Red, orange, fushia, and pink. She pulled the petals off the stems and nonchalantly threw them over her shoulder onto the tile floor. She carefully and meticulously cut each and every thorn off the stems. She pierced each thorn into a honeycomb and then dropped the dripping comb into the tub. The Warrior then slid into the water and scrubbed her body down with the thorn-laced comb. I don't know why she did this. My head was filled with a humming like the buzzing of bees. My heart was stung with a piercing ache and my powers of magical analysis suddenly failed me. All I could do was watch in breathless awe. Her glistening skin seemed to shimmer like gold. She emerged from the tub and trod upon all the rose petals strewn about the floor as if they were a carpet laid out for her. And then, with her skin still wet, she began to rub an oil into her body. (Unfortunately when I become invisible, I cannot wear my reading glasses, for they would give me away. So I couldn't quite make out this oil.) I believe it was coconut, which is for love and intuitiveness, although it may very well have been cottonseed, which draws information. The next step was correctly recorded by my ever-trusty nose. She carefully dabbed a concentrated potion of oil of clove in the outer corners of her eyes and the inner regions of her thighs. This gives her extraordinary vision and compels all who look at her legs to do her bidding. I have seen men fall at the feet of las Guerreras and blabber out top-secret business strategy, things they would normally only tell to other men.

I have seen the Warriors take the *agua de naranja de sangre en flor* to their breasts and splash the scent of blood-orange blossom over their mercenary hearts. I have then seen them trace along the outline of their cleavage to form the powerful letter *V*. They use the thumbs for this ritual as it is the digit sacred to the goddess Venus. Las Guerreras chant a sacred and powerful chant as they anoint their breasts. They chant deep in the throat and low under the breath but I have heard their words:

Venus de los viernes,
hazme victoriosa,

Vencedora y vitola.[1]
Haz que varones esclarecidos
me veneren y que vacilen.
Vacilar entre dos opciones
mi seno derecho y mi izquierdo,
vahidos de mi veneno sútil,
y revelarme todas sus verdades.
Soy vidente, una víbora ascendente.
Todas mis víctimas puedo vincular,
por la fuerza de mi voluntad,
y la viñeta de Venus.

I will translate them for you:

Venus of the Fridays,
make me victorious,
invincible, and good-looking.
Cause great men
to worship me, and to stumble.
To falter between two possibilities:
my right and left breasts.
To become dizzy from my subtle poison
and reveal to me all their truths.
I am a seer, an ascending viper.[2]
All my victims I am able to bind
by the strength of my will
and the vignette of Venus.

---

[1] At this point they often press a cigar band (*vitola*) over the thumb while chanting. VCentennial and Vegafina Torpedos are the favored brands.

[2] The meaning here might also be "my purse or money belt grows."

They allow the palms of their hands to graze their nipples as they trace down with their thumbs to form the vignette, or signature of Venus. They plunge deeply to reach the vortex, the point of the letter *V*, The thumbs meet at the vulva and press together to end the forming of the letter. Las Guerreras hold the thumbs pressed together at this supreme and sacred point until they feel the concentration of their power and the culmination of their prayer. They use nineteen words beginning with the letter *V* in their incantation. Nineteen is the kabalistic number of Eve. The letters of her Hebrew name add up to nineteen. Las Guerreras invoke all the power of Eve, the first woman, in her quest for knowledge and information, to cause the downfall of man. Before dressing, the Warriors turn and admire themselves in the mirror. They practice mudras[3] by pressing the thumbs and middle fingers together—the joining of power (Saturn) with seduction (Venus). They end the mudra with seven hard snaps between the thumbs and the middle fingers. They strike poses with apples held in their hands. Smiling they extend their arms as if to offer the fruit to a hungry man. Finally they bite into the apple with the sharpest of teeth. They eat the wise fruit to anoint their insides. Now they are ready to conquer and destroy (so that they can do good deeds)! They dress to kill. No man is safe from them. The Warriors' tactics are invincible. Some men see them coming and say ah, las Guerreras! But still they fall beneath their spell. There is no magic more powerful, more alluring, more deadly, more delightful.

---

[3]Mystical yoga position of the hands.

LIVING WELL SPELL

INGREDIENTS

grains and seeds

It is said that living well is the best revenge. An old proverb advises that it is better to make a wish for oneself than to curse another. I believe this. For those interested in another type of revenge, see Spell to Kill Your Boss. This spell is for those who have been seriously stung in a professional situation and are now seeking the ultimate revenge.

Saturn is known as the unlucky planet or the god who deals out harshness and restrictions. Saturn is also the ruler of the tenth house in astrology. The tenth house rules our professional status and reputation in the world. Oftentimes old Saturn will smack us around, deliver a harsh blow or a rotten deal of the cards. He will power-trip and pull the plug on our good fortune. He will often use nasty human representatives to accomplish his goals. When Saturn is through with us we may be scrambling to preserve whatever shreds of dignity we have left. We may be scrounging around to drum up cash to salvage our financial fortunes. We may be mad as hell and aching to get even while in the midst of struggling to repair our wounds. At this point it is wise to stay far away from nasty old Saturn. Do not try to boomerang his power, for it is likely to go into a tailspin and hit you even harder.

No, it is best to slyly seek the help of grouchy old Saturn's benevolent wife, the goddess Ops. The word *opulence* has its root in her name. She brings bounty and her name means "plenty." Ops is the goddess of sowing and reaping. So if you feel you've been dealt a bad hand, that you deserve more out of life, try getting even by getting opulent. Grains and seeds are the most sacred to Ops. The knuckles of the hands are very pleasing to her and in ancient times these bones were used to form the sacred rattles used in her processions. The most powerful rite to Ops involved touching the earth. So powerful was this ritual and the superstitions around it that during the medieval Inquisition many Church Fathers had witches lifted and carried to the prisons. It was believed that if the feet of these witches even so much as touched the ground, they would be empowered by the magic of their Goddess. I offer this simple yet most powerful ritual to summon the goddess Ops into your life so that you may live exceedingly well and therefore exact the best kind of revenge.

Stand outside under a full moon. Remove your shoes and stand barefoot upon the earth. Reach down into a bag you have brought with you and fill your hands with seeds and grains.* Pour them upon the earth to form a circle around yourself. Bend down and touch the earth with palms facing upward so that your knuckles are touching the ground. Chant:

> *I surround myself with the goodness of Ops,*
> *with prayer that she give me bountiful crops,*
> *Cybele, Ceres, Rhea,*
> *O sacred Bona Dea,*
> *by all the names that you were once known,*

---

*Poppy, pine needles, and bee pollen are also sacred to Ops. She loves the sound of cymbals, if you would like to use them with your chant.

by the power of my knucklebone.
O greatest goddess Ops, hear my cry,
let my enemies eat humble pie
when they witness the riches you bestow upon me.
Grant me your blessings of opulence, so mote it be.

NOTE: this spell is also recommended for farmers. It should be performed twice a year, December 19 and August 25, which are the sacred days of Ops. The chant should go as follows:

I surround myself with the goodness of Ops,
with prayer that she give me bountiful crops,
Cybele, Ceres, Rhea,
O sacred Bona Dea,
by all the names that you were once known,
by the power of my knucklebone.
O greatest goddess of Earth, Ops, hear my cry,
let my fields prosper under your watchful eye,
bestow your opulence unto me.
Grant me your blessings, so mote it be.

MERCHANTS, MILITARY LEADERS, AND SAINTS

INGREDIENTS

I.
90 coins
molasses

lime
cloves
cinnamon
yucca
tangerine
red carnation flowers
fresh milk
dirt from four churches

Nine and all dividends of nine are the sacred number of Oya. She is the Yoruban goddess of merchants. Place ninety pennies (or coins) in a bowl near the cash register and cover with thick molasses to draw constant money into your place of business. Every tenth coin should be silver (use a dime or a silver dollar) for extra prosperity. Ask Oya to help you bury your competition as she is also the goddess ruling the cemetery and death.

Oya is associated with the highest level of spirituality as well as the forces of battle and destruction. She is the goddess of all warriors. She can be summoned to protect soldiers and to bring military triumph. A martial talisman can be made for security and success with some of her sacred herbs. Stud a lime with cloves and cinnamon stick splinters for power, protection, and victory against adversaries. Carry this talisman in a pouch on your person when you go to war.

Because she is the ruler of death, (a state all potential saints must go through before attaining sainthood) Oya is the proper goddess to petition for sainthood. If you are serious about reaching this sublime level of spiritual elevation, prepare an offering to Oya. Slice open a yucca and fill its cavity with pulverized tangerine (flesh and rind), crushed red carnation flowers, four tablespoons of fresh milk, and a sprinkle of dirt from four churches.* Ask Oya to help you become a saint. (You may also pray to St. Catherine as she is a Christian counterpart of Oya.) There are three prime locations of power to connect with Oya and leave her offerings. The first is in front of a spinning or potters wheel. The second is outside in a lightning storm. The third is in a cemetery or in the company of the dying. And of course it is advisable to do good works for those about to cross over into the next world. The wheel, the lightning bolt, and the dying are all sacred to St. Catherine. The offering includes things most sacred to Oya.

INGREDIENTS

II.
Basil leaves

Placing a sprig of basil in a cash register is said to increase business. You can also make a tea or infusion of basil and add to your floor wash to mop the floor in your place of business. Or place the infusion in a spray bottle once it has cooled and spray the four corners in a clockwise direction. For those who do phone or door-to-door sales, eat basil on Tuesdays, Wednesdays, or Thursdays to increase your selling power.

Basil is also a sacred herb of military leaders and saints. A favored name of Byzantine emperors, the herb is believed

---

*The four churches must be located in the four corners of your city or town. One in the east, one in the south, west, and north ends of town.

to bring success in battle. Military leaders should follow the ancient custom of vigorously rubbing down the arms, shoulders, and legs with fresh basil sprigs before going to war. St. Basil is remembered for his hermitages at Mt. Athos and Mt. Sinai. He is known for justice and righting wrongs. If you are righteous enough to follow in his footsteps, place basil under your pillow. It is said that a sprig laid beneath a sleeping person will drive away all evil. Basil is also considered holy in more than one culture, and was believed to open the gates of heaven to the pious.

NETWORKING SPELL

INGREDIENTS

cinnamon powder
crushed dried rose petals
gold or copper glitter or sand

Mix all the ingredients in a bowl and then sprinkle on an altar or table in the form of an arrow pointing toward a picture of you or your business or a letterhead or résumé with your name on it. The idea is to stimulate and draw favorable energy, activity, people, and/or situations toward you. These ingredients are favorites of several love goddesses who are renowned for their powers of attraction and allure. If you were to perform the spell with red glitter or sand, it would attract romance. Gold or copper attracts success in business.

PHYSICIANS, NURSES, AND HEALERS

One of my most memorable recollections in the twenty-some years I have been serving the magical needs of the New York Wiccan community is that of a young woman who used to stop by to purchase healing herbs for her rituals. After she was accepted into medical school she disappeared for over a decade. About two years ago, she popped in again to buy some supplies. She is now an M.D. The doctor turned to me wistfully, and said: "Remember when I used to be a true and gifted healer—*before* I got accepted into medical school?!!"

Unfortunately science and spirituality are still far from becoming bedfellows. In the days before the AMA, medicine was strictly a business belonging to religion and religious orders. In more recent times, religion and spirituality were ousted from the practice of medicine and replaced by facts. Facts and research lead to knowledge, which is not synonymous with wisdom. Wisdom is something that is gleaned from the utilization and experience of the whole. Research has shown that prayer has an enormous effect on healing. My feeling is that prayer should be utilized by the physician as well as the patient. When only one-half of the party is calling in the divine spirit, there is bound to be a blockage of energy.

What follows is a sacred chant to the healing gods and

goddesses of antiquity. They are still very much alive. They still survive symbolically in the modern world, however many have forgotten what and who their powerful symbols actually stand for.

This chant or prayer can be used by anyone in the field of medicine (traditional or alternative) to invoke healing powers. In the tradition of "Physician heal thyself" these chants can also be used by anyone needing to improve his or her health. The prayer is used to invoke healing energy into the body. It can also be used to temper the effects of becoming jaded, a situation that can happen in any profession. (In fact, I have a general spell to offset the effects of becoming jaded, but this particular spell is specifically for those in the medical field. The profession of saving lives is a sacred one and it is most important for those involved to be aligned with the healing forces of the divine.) This chant can also be used by the medical practitioner who has become burned out by seeing too much, or losing patients, or just losing touch with their spiritual reasons for choosing this field.

The litany is written for the Greek goddesses Hygeia and Panacea and the Greek god Asklepios. The goddesses were said to be the twin milk-filled breasts of the mother goddess Rhea. Panacea was believed to possess the power to cure all ailments. Hygeia was the guardian of physical as well as mental health, and also protected one from danger. She was depicted as a kind maiden feeding a serpent from a dish. This was the sacred serpent who shed his skin (representing rejuvenation) and wrapped him/herself around the rod. Eventually Hygeia was made the daughter of Asklepios, (Asklepios—Greek/Æsculapius—Latin) as was the fate of most goddesses during the patriarchal takeover. They became the daughters and wives of the gods.

Asklepios was the son of Apollo and Coronis. Asklepios worship in Phoenicia and Egypt spread to Greece and Rome. He was known as such a great healer that he even had the power to raise people from the dead. He was stopped from doing this work because the underworld became underpopulated as a result. The sacred symbol of Asklepios was the caduceus, the winged staff with the twin serpents wrapped around it or sometimes a single serpent wrapped around a staff. The AMA adopted the caduceus as their calling card, however they seem to have forgotten some of the healing truths of Asklepios. It is believed that Asklepios transmitted his healing powers by curing the astral body or by visiting the sick in their dreams. Once the astral body was touched by his staff, the healing energy would then enter the patient's physical body.

If we examine recent phenomena such as the APA's overuse of pharmaceuticals instead of talk therapy to cure the soul, the AMA's political assassination of vitamins and herbal or Ayurvedic cures, the bias against faith healers and Reiki practitioners, it seems clear that the tendency to take care of the astral body or soul has fallen by the wayside. The popular belief seems to be that if you can't find it in a test tube, it must not exist. The tides are turning in the twenty-first century, but they move at a snail's pace.

The recitation of this chant or litany on a daily basis can also help to create a balance between spiritual healing and medicine. I will not deny that the scales have often tipped over and caused horrible spills with charlatans and faith healers playing off the desperation of sick people. Those people may die needlessly by not heeding the words of medical doctors, whose scientific procedure could have easily prolonged their lives. This is why the balance becomes essential. The merging of the care of body and soul will ultimately provide the most effective forms of well being.

Panacea and Hygeia,
twin breasts of the goddess Rhea,
feeders of the sacred serpent,
sustainers of life so fervent.
You who heal all; the vital milk of the goddess
guard me from dis-ease and strife.
Bless me with curative powers
to create, preserve, sustain, and nurture life.

I summon you, Asklepios.
Please teach me how to diagnose,
O great curing god who carries the rod.
Let the sacred art of healing flow through my hands.
Let my work be guided by your immortal plans.
Bring insight, intuition back to my field.
Thy wisdom, thy power, thy healing arts yield.
Consecrate me with your staff,
a healer on your behalf.

NOTE: Is your job at risk because of too many sick days? This spell can also be used to heal yourself and get yourself back to work. It can also be used to negotiate more sick days if that is what you truly need. Use the spell to summon health insurance or benefits on a job. If you have been injured or cannot work because of health reasons, use this spell/chant to negotiate your financial terms. Hold a bay leaf and a sprig of basil in your hand while chanting when money settlements are desired for health issues.

POWER PUNCH

INGREDIENTS

mango
lime

For those who need to pack a powerful punch in their professional lives, this is a potion originally designed for professional boxers, but which can be used by anyone in a cutthroat business who needs to have a powerful edge.

Drink fresh mango and lime juice first thing in the morning, before ingesting any other food or drink, or eat the fruit of a mango with fresh lime slices.

Lime and mango summon power and stamina. They can also help to control or regulate your flow of energy. Sometimes you may need to save your best punch for the last round. Other times you may need to come out swinging right from the top.

PRESERVATION SPELL

INGREDIENTS

chunk light tuna
salt and pepper
dash of lemon juice
olive oil
canned carrots, corn, beets
Spanish olives
pickles
iceberg lettuce

This spell is used for preservation. Do you need to hang on to something? Do you feel or sense that what you have achieved is in danger of being lost? Use this spell if you have achieved success but feel it is threatened by jealousy or sabotage. The spell can be used by anyone, successful or not, who feels the need for refuge or shelter. All canned goods have the magical property of maintaining and protecting. Never use fresh ingredients in this spell, except for the lettuce. Please do use fresh lettuce!

Iceberg lettuce can be used to camouflage, to hide you from danger, to make your assets, material and spiritual, not stand out and be noticed in a negative way. Sometimes our success needs to be protected and hidden from jealous and vengeful eyes. Iceberg lettuce is considered common. It is not as fancy or nutritious as the darker lettuces. Therefore the use of it can tone down others' negative perceptions or jealousies of you. It makes you appear more ordinary. Pickles are mercurial and will help you to shift and reposition yourself in order to maintain. They also stimulate creativity and promote good communication. Corn is a staple food representing continuous prosperity. Beets and olive oil preserve and bring longevity. Green olives are specifically used to preserve and protect income. Carrots add perception and depth for troubleshooting. Salt and lemon purify and protect, and salt summons prosperity. Pepper repels enemies. Tuna and all fish lend serious protection by hiding you from harm's way.

Prepare this as a salad and eat at any time, during any moon phase. Most importantly, prepare it when you feel your success is threatened by inner or outer influences. There's no telling what the results may be. If there is negative energy being "canned" up, this spell may release it. It may be possible that your preservation is dependent upon radical change. It may also be possible that maintaining the status quo is integral to your preservation. You must be open to any possibility before performing this spell. And you must be willing to trust that the gods will catch you no matter where you fall. Be forewarned, seven out of twenty-five people who performed this spell, lost their jobs after doing so, (myself included). However all seven weathered the change quite successfully and are in much better positions financially and emotionally now.

You cannot predict the exact outcome of this spell, it is a tricky one. I can only say that if you invoke a storm, you will weather it, and find yourself in a safe and calm port. Sometimes life has to come undone in order to better provide for and protect us. So be it.

PROTECTION ON THE JOB SPELL

INGREDIENTS

dried lemon peel
coarse salt
bay leaves
green pepper seeds
bergamot (Earl Grey tea)
clove
cinnamon powder
ginger powder

This spell is to be used if you feel your job may be placing you in serious or life-threatening danger. The spell was originally designed for law enforcement professionals. In my twenty years of magical counseling, the most consistent request from police officers and firemen was for protection spells. So I offer a strong and potent one here.

Lemon, salt, bay, and green pepper all contain protective vibrations. To combine them creates a very strong shield of defense. Bergamot is used to prevent any sudden accidents or movements that might cause you harm. Clove, cinnamon, and ginger combined create more of an aggressive type of armor for those who need to work on the offensive. All ingredients should be ground to a fine powder and mixed together. The powder can be placed in the shoes, sprinkled around the place of work, or carried in a pouch on your person for safety and protection.

REAL ESTATE SPELL

Throughout the history of magic, human secretions have played a very mystical role. There are countless spells and rituals that include the use of the alchemical fluids (blood, semen, and urine). The blood lore continues to thrive through the vampire cults. Worship of as well as taboos concerning the male seed and the menses permeate both ancient and modern culture. Urine therapy, or the practice of drinking one's own urine for healing purposes, has become very popular as of late. I suppose if I were stranded in the Himalayas I would drink my own urine, but not before I tried nettle tea. In general my beverages of choice are Champagne, Campari, orange juice, coffee, yerba maté, good old H_2O and I've always Got Milk. That is not to say that I disapprove of or judge people who drink their own urine for its therapeutic value. I understand it has many healing attributes. There have already been books written on this subject, if you, dear reader, care to investigate further.

I mean only to peer into the matter in order to explain another strain of magic using the golden elixir. It is a powerful form of animal energy that I call territorial magic. An animal will place its scent around an area to secure that space as its own. Cats do this by spraying or marking. Spraying uses an actual body fluid that is shot out from behind the tail. Marking can be done by rubbing the face against an area to secrete a scent hidden behind the whiskers. Marking can also be done by using the claws. The best way for humans to mark or scent is through the use of urine. There are many ancient witchcraft spells involving the use of urine to secure something. It is mostly used in protection magic— sometimes in cursing, or for love. But its most powerful attributes are in creating and marking boundaries.

One day a client of mine named Nell came to see me in a total panic. She was illegally subletting a rent-stabilized apartment. Nell was terrified that she would lose the apartment and was desperately trying to take over the lease again. I suggested that she visualize her safety and security in the flat every single morning with the first pee of the day. I told her to begin the ritual with visualization on the new moon and to carry it through till the full moon. That's fourteen days of property peeing. I also told Nell to consecrate the four corners of her apartment with flour and sage to bless and protect it. I did however fail to point out to Nell that this ritual should be performed *in the bathroom*. I thought that would be taken for granted. Nervous Nell peed in the four corners of her apartment for fourteen days! I guess nothing should be taken for granted.

Let me just clarify for my readers at this point that this spell is meant to be performed *in the bathroom*. *Over the toilet bowl.* You got that?! This is a modern, civilized ritual. You should pee as you normally pee except that you must think about the security of your dwelling, or about securing a particular dwelling, as you urinate. The release of this very magical bodily fluid along with forming mental pictures will help you manifest a space.

Suppose you are looking to buy or rent a particular property for business or personal reasons; you simply *ask the real estate agent if you may use the toilet* while you are there. If possible go back again, (at least three times between a new and full moon) go to the bathroom, and as you urinate, visualize yourself signing the lease, getting approved by the board, moving in your stuff, etc. This ritual can be highly effective when there is competition over obtaining a space. It is meant to be performed on properties that already contain working plumbing.

If you are purchasing land, I suppose it is okay to take a little piss in the woods when no one is looking. However with land, it is actually more effective to call out your name while sprinkling a pack of seeds upon the ground. Spit (the fourth alchemical fluid) three times upon the seeds and then use your foot to cover them with earth. It is believed that when the seeds begin to sprout, the property will be yours or the property will become fertile ground for you. You could hardly perform a ritual like that with any degree of success in an apartment with terra cotta tile floors, or an office with wall-to-wall carpeting. But you could go into the green marble bathroom, do your thing, and confidently see the place as yours.

This whizzing ritual can also be used in competitive work situations. A salesman I know felt that another company was moving in on his turf. He held a map of the northeastern United States in his free hand as he urinated in the toilet.

He did this for fourteen days, from the full to new moon,* and sure enough, his competition backed off those territories. I'm telling you, this pissing spell works.

Oh, and as for Nell, that was actually a fierce piss o' magic she worked. The apartment is hers. Not only did she get a lease but an option to buy, at insider's price. The apartment is now hers for life, along with an interesting side effect: her roof leaks above the four corners every time it rains.

In primitive cultures it was believed that rain was caused by the gods urinating upon the earth. Early fertility rites were performed by priests urinating upon the body of a woman or priestess. She represented Mother Earth. In later times, a differentiation was made between urine and semen. Then the fertility rites were practiced through the *hieros gamos*, or sacred marriage, the sexual union of king and priestess representing union of god and goddess. It is my belief that Nell, with her primal urgency, tapped into the oldest form of the magic. The four corners are also symbolic of Mother Earth. I am glad to report that Nell happily reigns even through the rain. She has set four large flower pots under the four wet spots, containing ivy, lavender, rosemary, and fern, all very protective and prosperous plants to grow in the home. The herbs are thriving. Nell may forget to water them, but not the gods.

---

*This man chose to work the waning moon cycle as he was trying to rid the area of his competitors. Normally the spell would be worked during the waxing cycle in order to obtain or gain the space.

SCHEDULING SPELL

INGREDIENTS

wintergreen leaves
yellow rose petals
lemon peel
celery seed

This spell is used to help solve scheduling problems. Are you a director or stage manager pulling your hair out trying to get twelve actors to meet? An airline stewardess bidding for that flight to Paris next Friday morning with the layover till Monday? Are you having trouble making appointments? Worried about the vacation time you requested being approved? Or are you trying to transfer to a specific location? This spell is to remedy all those problems having to do with time or location scheduling.

The combined ingredients create what we witches call an As You Please, Friendly Persuasion, or Bend Over formula. These are all popular blends with mild elements of control. Mercury is the dominant ruler of the formula, so the emphasis is on clear communication and success.

Simply write down your name and what you want (including dates and/or location). Include names of any other persons involved. Sprinkle a mixture of dried wintergreen leaves, dried yellow rose petals, dried lemon peel, and celery seed to completely cover the request. You can also carry these herbs in your pocket when going to petition for your time or location.

Add fennel seeds if what you need is more flexibility between people. Fennel is sacred to the mutable astrological signs.

Add cinnamon if you need a push into action. Cinnamon is sacred to the cardinal astrological signs. It should be used when there is too much talk about getting together and you need to just *do it!*

Add sesame seeds when you need people to revolve around you and your schedule. Sesame is sacred to the fixed signs and will help you to be the unmovable, nonnegotiable center. It can also be added to stop scheduling problems that occur because of erratic behavior.

SELF-ESTEEM AND SELF-CONFIDENCE SPELL

INGREDIENTS

cherry pie
powdered nutmeg

My copy editor has informed me that the connection of an Old English word from the Middle Ages to Greek mathematics is *extremely* dubious, and unsubstantiated by either OED or Webster's. Yet, my psychic sense and overactive imagination, which insists on stretching the truth, tells me that the word *pie* got its name from the mathematical term pi (π), because in Roman times the dish contained a jumble of things (mostly meat or fish) within the circumference of a circle (or pie crust). Queen Elizabeth I was the first to request a dessert or fruit pie. Her desire was for pitted and preserved cherries to be baked in a pie.

Is your head jumbled up with information and advice from others? Are you chasing your tail trying to satisfy everyone else while ignoring your own intuitive sense of where you should be headed? Follow the suit of a woman who knew her own mind. The reign of Queen Elizabeth I brought England to its greatest glory. Eat cherry pie when you need to trust yourself above all others. Sprinkle the cherry pie with a hint of powdered nutmeg. Cherries promote self-confidence, nutmeg increases intuition. The combination of the two will help you to have the certainty and conviction to follow your own instincts, to trust yourself above all others. The mixture is also said to reinvigorate personal joy in one's work.

SHADE SPELLS

INGREDIENTS

sunglasses
lemon rind
black shoelace
charcoal

I. Have you lost some business because of your poor negotiation skills? Do you have a face that reveals all? This spell is to help you achieve the unreadable poker face. It will enable you to lie and go undetected, to sit in a meeting and absorb all information with no one being able to read which side you are on. No one will know if you are bluffing either.

Sunglasses were first worn in fourteenth-century China by judges so that their eyes would not reveal where their sympathies lay. The sunglasses allowed them to appear to be impartial. I do not advise walking into a contract negotiation wearing sunglasses unless the meeting is taking place outdoors on a sunny day. Otherwise you may be off-putting. However you can still use sunglasses as a magical talisman to hide the giveaway expressions on your face.

Before your meeting, dip the sunglasses in a mixture of lemon rind ground to a fine powder, the ashes of a knotted and burnt black shoelace, and charcoal powder. These ingredients are a traditional witches' brew used to protect, hide, and obscure. Dip the glasses in the mixture, and say:

> My true thoughts are in disguise.
> Let none see behind my eyes,
> made blank with lemon, ash, and coal.
> My face does not reveal my goal.

Place the sunglasses on your face for fifteen minutes. Stand quietly, empty the mind, close the eyes, and relax the face. Remove glasses and wipe any powder residue off the face before entering your meeting. The effects should last up to five hours. Repeat when necessary.

II. Some other interesting notes about the magical properties of sunglasses: mirrored shades can be used to deflect the
evil eye or jealousy. Wear mirrored sunglasses when con-
fronting enemies or those who wish you harm. You can also
place the mirrored sunglasses in a breast pocket to deflect
negative energy. These words can be spoken:

> *Reflective ray, keep away*
> *the evil glance cast my way.*
> *Mirror it back before it touch*
> *or harm or maim.*
> *Let it triple attack the eye*
> *from whence it came.*

Your sender of bad energy should back off once he or
she has had a magnified look at the nastiness that came from
behind his or her own eyes.

III. In the 1960s with the famous Foster Grant commer-
cials, wearing sunglasses suggested movie star status. To
glamorize your shades, prepare a mixture of roseflower water
and orange blossom water with a sprinkle of thyme, star
anise, and poppy seeds. This combination is said to create
charisma, allure, and illusion. Dip a soft cloth in this potion
and rub the lenses while chanting:

> *Conjure, draw and captivate.*
> *I wish to simply fascinate.*
> *Recognize me from afar.*
> *Behind these shades stands a great star.*

I personally tried this last spell on two separate occasions. On the first I was surrounded by a group of construction workers who were convinced that I was Madonna. They would not let me go until I signed my name (Madonna's name) in a block of wet cement. On the second outing I found myself surrounded by a gaggle of girls who were quite sure, completely convinced, that I was Sean Penn. They would not let me go until I planted kisses on all their lips. I did however threaten to punch the one holding a camera. (Just trying to keep in character.) I highly recommend this spell to anyone trying to get work as a stand-in, to all professional Elvis impersonators, and to anyone who makes a living as a look-alike.

SPELL FOR FULFILLMENT IN WORK

INGREDIENTS

ground ginger
ground orange peel
dried basil leaves

This mixture should be used to dust the hands before working or should be sprinkled around the place of work. The main purpose of this formula is to create both happiness and financial fulfillment. Many people must work at jobs to pay their bills but find that the actual work is so unfulfilling that they suffocate their souls in order to feed their bellies.

Use this potion to find happiness and spiritual gratification in your job.

Ginger helps to create change. Basil banishes bad luck and bad energy but is also used to attract money and recognition. Orange is purely for love and fulfillment. The combination of all three will attract creative and loving ways to earn money.

SPELL FOR RENEWAL

INGREDIENTS

ten whole uncooked eggs
parsley

Do you feel as if you've lost your touch? Getting old, worn out, dried up? Uninspired? Need to rid yourself of weight and fear? Soak in a tub of warm water with ten whole unbroken raw eggs. Let them lie around in the tub with you. Add a large bunch of fresh parsley and rub your body down with the parsley as you float in the eggs. Eggs have the magical ability to pull negativity out of the body. They are also symbols of renewal. Parsley refreshes and invigorates. Take this bath on a new moon to help revitalize your dreams, goals, and career plans.

SPELL TO DRAW CLIENTS

INGREDIENTS

mangoes
molasses
dark rum

Hindus use the mango as a symbol of prosperity. In Hawaiian lore, to dream of a mango means money is coming. In Central America, the fruit is believed to excite the senses. Although usually associated with sexual attraction, mango can serve as a money-drawing agent as well. Molasses is used to draw and compel. Its scorpionic traits make molasses serve as an irresistible drawing agent. Molasses is also sacred to the Yoruban goddess Oya, who is the patron saint of merchants. Dark rum is given as offerings to Ellegua, the god who removes obstacles and clears the path. It is also a favorite of Chango, a god associated with business and commerce.

To draw clients into a store or place of business, peel the skin from a mango and place the fruit in a bowl. Drizzle a generous amount of molasses onto the fruit and pour or spit a shot of dark rum over the mango. Place the bowl by the door of your business. Leave out until the fruit begins to rot. Dispose of properly and repeat on the next new moon. If you need to draw clients to yourself, as opposed to a space, blend a potion made of mango juice, a teaspoon of molasses, and a shot of rum. Drink or add to your bathwater.

SPELL TO GET MOTIVATED

orange bell pepper
crushed eggshell
sage
lavender
rose petals
ginger
bay
lemon
vanilla

This spell is used to create more self-motivation, ambition, and drive to accomplish tasks and fulfill goals. The ingredients are sacred to the Seven African Powers who are often called upon to cleanse and uncross us on all levels so that we are able to operate at our full and energized potential.

Remove the seeds from an orange bell pepper and allow them to dry. Count out forty-nine seeds. Forty-nine is the number of strength and determination. Crack open an egg (you may dispose of the egg or cook and eat it), rinse the empty shell, and also allow it to dry. Using a mortar and pestle, crush the eggshell to a fine powder. Combine powdered sage, lavender, dried red and yellow rose petals, powdered ginger, crushed bay leaves, and dried lemon peel in a mixing bowl. Stir in the pepper seeds and eggshell powder. Add seven drops of pure vanilla extract and mix well. Sniff the potion as an aromatherapy to get you going. You can also sew the powder up in a red silk cloth using yellow thread and carry and rub as a talisman when you need help getting motivated.

Sage, lavender, and lemon clear the mind and alleviate stress. Eggshell renews our energy. Orange peppers and ginger command us into action. Rose and vanilla promote self-love and self-confidence. Bay is used for victory.

SPELL TO KEEP YOUR PANTS ON

INGREDIENTS

I.
coriander
cumin
marjoram
caraway seeds
sage
senna leaves

II.
black or purple veil
pomegranate
palm kernel oil

It seems as if every other day (as in Monday, Wednesday, Friday, Sunday, Tuesday, Thursday, and Saturday!) another politician is caught with his pants down. The close of the

millennium brought a storm of sex scandals that destroyed
or at least badly damaged several political careers. I offer up
these two spells to help you control your sexual appetite
and/or guard your reputation.

I. In order to perform this first spell you actually need to
take your pants off (ha-ha). It's best if you use an old pair
of trousers you are willing to part with. Stuff the pants
pockets with coriander, cumin, marjoram, caraway seeds,
sage, and senna leaves. Each of these herbs is used individ-
ually to stop infidelity. Combined they all increase in power
and should be strong enough to control those big political
libidos. With a needle and black thread sew the pockets and
the fly of the pants shut. Use double stitching, please. Then
triple knot the pant legs so that you now have a huge knot
in the crotch of the pants. Sprinkle more herbs upon this
triple knot and drip the wax of a red candle over the herbs
and knotted crotch of the pants. Red symbolizes control.
Throw these pants in a pillowcase and place under your bed,
under your desk, or carry on the road with you to prevent
sexual misconduct. This spell can be performed by the individual who needs help, by the wife of this individual, or
by the political advisor of this individual. The spell will be
effective in all cases.

II. It is said that the more powerful the man, the more
powerful his libido. I believe this is true. This second spell
is for those of you who don't see your active sex life as the
problem. The problem, as you see it, is *getting caught!* The
palm and the pomegranate are the sacred symbols of the
High Priestess of the tarot. She is the guardian of all secrets,

especially sexual ones. To keep the media from piercing your veil of privacy, write your name on the face of a pomegranate during the dark of the moon. Anoint this pomegranate with palm oil and wrap it in a veil of purple or black. (The veil is also sacred to the High Priestess.) Keep this talisman with you when you want to fool around but *always* make sure it is hidden from others.

SPELL TO KILL YOUR BOSS

INGREDIENTS

9 eggplants
9 boxes of toothpicks
oven mitt
today's newspaper
combat boots

The modern religion of Wicca, which has been greatly influenced by Judeo-Christian values, strongly advocates a hands-off, turn-the-other-cheek, do-what-ye-will-yet-harm-none approach to magic. I myself have reminded my readers of this in past books as well as warning them of the old law of karma that whatever you do will come back at you three- or tenfold times. And I still believe that it is good to practice these rules, or at least consider them carefully before you act on a magical level.

However I also think that the original practice of good old-fashioned witchcraft contained a lot of good old-fashioned downright vexatious spells. Scary stuff. Why else do you think the medieval inquisitors burned so many of those witches? Because they were Pollyannas in ruby slippers?[1] No way. It was because they were badass babes— provocative and powerful, wonderfully wicked wisenheimers! Another saying of the witches that is not spoken as loudly as Do what ye will . . . is A witch who can't hex, can't heal. That's right. Sometimes you just gotta flaunt your stuff. So if you feel the need—hex away!

I also want to point out that in the numerous interviews I conducted in order to write this book, this spell was the number-one request. It was asked for by men and women in all types of professions. There were even two requests from people who were self-employed! (Huh?!) I myself worked for a repulsive hag of a boss for years, not to mention having to put up with jealous and incompetent witch wannabes as co-workers. So what do you say we put on our inquisitor hats[2] and burn these bosses at the stake?

Some more words before we begin. If you have just been fired or want to quit because you hate your boss so bad, it is probably imperative that you perform this spell. Otherwise you might become a homicidal maniac and act out in a real-world way that could ruin your life and land you in jail. Believe me, you don't want to do that. Matters such as these are much better performed in the magical realm. Don't waste your life by really killing your boss. If you hate him or her that badly, I am quite convinced that he or she must be a completely miserable, horrible person. Getting fired by or quitting working for this boss will be a blessing (not even

---

[1] That means "a bunch of Goody Two-shoes"!

[2] Or should we wear pointy wicked-witch hats?

in disguise) for you. Better that you get out of the quagmire, for it is only a matter of time before someone like your boss comes toppling down because of his or her own dirty deeds. Why not just do a little magic to hasten the inevitable? ...

Now for the spell. Obtain nine small eggplants. Nine is the number of endings and eggplants are symbolic of death. Stuff a whole box of toothpicks in each of the eggplants and call out all the curses you wish to fall upon your boss as you prick the eggplants with the wooden pins. These toothpicks are fuel for the fire. They represent little yet powerful stakes. (So many things at stake. Especially your sanity.) After you have sufficiently cursed each and every eggplant, place them all in the oven and set it on broil. Remember how badly you've been burned by this bad boss. Send all that heat back from whence it came. Roast the eggplants for about ninety minutes until they are thoroughly toasty and grilled. No, wait, until they are completely charred!

Let them cool slightly while you put on a pair of steel tipped combat boots. Spread the obituary section of today's paper on the counter. Using gloves or an oven mitt, remove the eggplants and lay them over the obits. Roll or fold up the paper with the eggplants inside. Go outdoors and place the parcel on the ground. Pound the f—k out of them with your combat boots. Grind them into the ground until they become a pulpy, harmless mush. End the ritual by rolling up the newspaper and burying it in a trashcan or Dumpster.(I don't think this boss deserves proper funeral rites.) Follow up by taking a bath in saltwater to purify yourself and eat a hardboiled egg to symbolize your wonderful new beginning.

Now, if the gods are good you may hear some "tragic" news about your boss. Something along the lines of the "terrible" news we heard here in NYC about someone who had been lording over the good citizens of Manhattan for years. This news was so "bad" that it stopped him from advancing himself to a national level of government. I'm not saying witchcraft had anything to do with that. I'm not saying it didn't either. All I'm saying is you may or may not hear of any "tragic" news concerning your boss. That is up to the gods. But I guarantee you will have a good old-fashioned healing, cathartic, cleansing, and empowering experience in those combat boots!

SPELL TO MAKE GOOD TIPS

INGREDIENTS

cinnamon sticks
vanilla extract
wintergreen extract

This is a very simple and effective spell to make bigger and better tips. The talismans should be prepared beforehand and carried in the pocket while on the job. Whittle a cinnamon stick into tiny little toothpicks. Dip them in a mixture of pure vanilla and pure wintergreen extracts. Let them stand and dry. Take these little toothpicks to work and carry in the pocket. Pop one in your mouth and chew while you work.

Cinnamon brings fast luck and is used to attract money. Vanilla pleases, and if you please, you will be rewarded. Wintergreen attracts friendly "green" or nature spirits to assist you. Wintergreen also makes people remember you. The combination of all three is used to make people happy with your service and remember to reward you financially.

SPELL TO QUIT HORSIN' AROUND

INGREDIENTS

star anise
sage
clove

Does your romantic partner not understand or accept your putting your work before your relationship? Is s/he competing for your attention? Are you losing energy struggling to attend to both your personal and business needs? Or are you screwing up at work because you've got your head in the clouds dreaming about a fella or a dame? If the answers to any of these questions are yes, you need this spell.

Roy Rogers frequently paid more attention to his horse than to his romantic interest. Roy put his horse before his lover because it made more sense. Dollars and cents! I also think this is why Roy has been a lot more successful than you or I with leaving his footprints in the sands of time.

It's just impossible to get any lasting work done when you've got a *boom-boom* in your head, in your heart, or down your pants. Just impossible!

Cloves clear the head, drive away distraction, and ease jealousy. They also attract riches.* Sage is for wisdom and is used to tone down the sexual drive. Star anise is used to create more understanding from a mate. It also enables you to become more centered in yourself. It brings awareness of the whole body, not just the sex organs. It is important to select a piece that is whole with all five points of the star intact. All three ingredients will clear and expand the mind. They are ruled by Sagittarius, whose totem is the hard-working horse. Sagittarius is also the Archer and teaches us how to take aim, stay focused, and reach our mark. It is the sign that follows Scorpio. Scorpio rules sexuality and the genitalia; the survival instinct of the human race to perpetuate itself through procreation, and all behavior that accompanies that, such as courting, mating, etc. The biological urge to reproduce is a deep and powerful force often operating on a subconscious level. Sagittarius teaches us that life is also sustained through forward movement and development of the human race by its philosophy and mental pursuits. Sagittarius represents departure and freedom from the biological urges. It offers instead the insight that the continuation of the race can also be fulfilled through personal accomplishment and positive changes in the human condition.

Imagine it this way: With Scorpio in charge, babies would

---

*Just be careful, for when clove is worn on the thighs it becomes highly sexual and seductive.

be born indiscriminately, regardless of whether or not they were healthy and born into families that could properly care for them. Sagittarius, on the other hand, would represent a discovery such as the identifying of the Rh-negative factor through the rhesus monkey, the detection of which evolved into the development of the drug Rhogam to prevent children from being born with mental retardation and serious birth defects. This greatly improved the quality of life. Sagittarius would also provide foster care for abandoned children. Sagittarius prepares and teaches us to travel toward the tenth house, or Capricorn. Capricorn represents our personal accomplishments, what we leave or give to the world through our deeds as opposed to our eggs and seeds.

This spell can also be used by those who are living in the shadow of their parents' achievements. It will help you to grow and attain something on your own. Individuation is achieved through Gemini, the third house. By using Sagittarius, the opposite end of the wheel, we can bring awareness to third-house matters.

Make a tea of clove, star anise, and sage. Drink on Thursdays during any moon phase. The herbs can also be carried dry in the pocket. You can also make an inhaler by placing drops of clove oil on star anise buttons and sage leaves. Think of Roy and trigger yourself into work mode. Go out and make something of yourself. Don't worry. Be confident. Your loved ones will be proud and waiting for you when you come home.

SPELLS FOR FAME

INGREDIENTS

I.
basil
sun-dried tomato
pine nuts
olives and or olive oil
a hint of garlic
angel-hair pasta

Is your destiny to become an Elenora Duse, a Garbo, a Gable, a Marilyn Monroe, an Isadora Duncan, Pablo Picasso, a Melville or Molière, Neruda, Madonna, Maria Callas, Lanza, or a Lennon (Lenin)? This spell will help to accelerate your rise to fame.

Basil not only attracts money and luck but love and fame. It is an ideal magical ingredient for those whose success depends on their popularity or public acclaim. Basil is also associated with vitality, charisma, and physical strength. I recommend its use for dancers, acrobats, or any performer who wishes to increase these attributes in him/herself. The tomato is sacred to Venus, but the sun-dried tomato represents Venus, the goddess of love, kissed by Apollo, the god of the arts. So the sun-dried tomato holds charismatic powers and can be used to attract the love and adoration of many people as opposed to just one. Sun-dried tomatoes are excellent for attracting fans and admirers. Pine nuts are another money/love double. Ruled by Mars, they also increase ambition and drive. A hint of garlic is used to increase sexuality and seduction. Garlic is the master of the wooing arts. Now, popularity and charm go only so far without real talent. In the words of Sharon Stone, "You can only sleep your way to the middle!" The olive is sacred to Apollo and in addition to representing long life and good health it also represents the spirituality and mysticism of the dramatic arts. Use olive oil to grease the wheels of your raw talent. Nuts in general promote talk amongst people. The combination of pine nuts and olive oil is said to promote continual talk about art or an artist. Pasta is ruled by Mercury, the god of speech, communication, and creativity. Angels are obviously symbols of the divine. It is believed that disorderly hair is a sign of immortality. Unless you can comb and untangle your angel-hair pasta it is a sure sign that your fame will last.

Boil sun-dried tomatoes to soften. Let cool and grind together with pine nuts, olive oil, three garlic cloves, and fresh chopped basil until it reaches a pastelike consistency (or buy a pesto sauce with sun-dried tomatoes). Mix into angel hair pasta on Wednesdays, Fridays, and/or Sundays. Visualize yourself becoming famous.

INGREDIENTS

II.
oranges
honey
figs

This spell is recommended for those working in media, film, stage, or television but it can also be used by anyone (in any profession) seeking attention and acclaim within their field. It can also be used to gain positive media attention or to make sure your own advertising or promotion plans are successful in the public eye.

Oranges and honey are sacred to Oshun, the goddess ruling love and drama. Figs also promote love, and combined with orange and honey they can help to generate the love of many as opposed to the love of just one. Eat oranges and fresh figs dipped in honey on the first Friday of the new moon to attract love of the masses. Visualize your goal and ask Oshun for her help as you eat. You must prepare a bowl of five oranges and five fresh figs drizzled with honey for Oshun after she has granted your request. Leave the offering out until mold appears on the oranges. This is a sign of Oshun accepting her offering. You may then dispose of the remains. Remember, you must taste all food before offering to Oshun or else she will not accept it.

SPONGE SPELL

INGREDIENTS

a sponge

The sponge, because of its porous nature, is a very magical tool. Use it to "wring yourself out" of excess negative energy. Use it to prevent psychic or emotional burnout and to release negative energy you have absorbed from others. Psychics, ER staff, psychotherapists, massage therapists, criminal lawyers, waitresses, or any professional who is in danger of absorbing negative energy from clients can benefit from the sponge technique. It can also be used by anyone who suffers distraction or stress in their work. A gray or black sponge, if you can find one, is best for neutralizing negative energy. Yellow is good for getting rid of distraction, and pink alleviates stress.

Take a sponge and hold it under running water. When the sponge soaks up the water wring it out with both hands. As you wring the water from the sponge imagine wringing out the negative energy you have absorbed. Or imagine scattered unfocused energy being wrung out. Repeat this three times while saying: "I wring out all distracting thoughts from my mind. I am no longer overwhelmed. I am able to focus on the task at hand." Or, "I release any and all negative energy I have absorbed during my work with (fill in name of client). I cleanse and release and neutralize so that I may be renewed."

For severe cases of mental anguish or mental confusion or distraction that keep you from focusing on your task, fill the sponge with water and wring out over your head. In cases where you do not have a sink available on the job, or time to wring sponges between clients, do the technique mentally. Visualization is a higher form of magic. It is hard to achieve. For most people the physical act of ritual is very important. Nonetheless it may be impractical to wring water over your head. Verbalizing during visualization is a way to compensate when you're not able to really do the action. Call out the distractions and see yourself being wrung free of them.

SUMMONING THE MUSES

The muses can be summoned to overcome writer's block or any creative block. Their presence is sure to bring more creativity and inspiration into your work. You may want to summon an individual muse to help you with a specific line of work. Here is a list of the nine muses and some ideas on how to court them for creative success:

Clio should be summoned by historians or those wishing to be remembered throughout history. Perhaps you just want to change or make some history in your own office—or maybe you are more ambitious and aspiring toward getting your own episode on *Biography*. Either way, Clio is the muse to summon. She is reported to love the scent of cinnamon, lemon, and orange. Burn incense in these three flavors or prepare a bowl of crushed cinnamon sticks, dried orange and lemon peel, and place on your worktable or in pocket, and sniff regularly. You can also rub your temples with a potion made of cinnamon, orange, and lemon extracts to summon her spirit into your mind.

Euterpe is the muse of flute music and poetry. She is most helpful to musicians and lyricists. To summon Euterpe obtain a length of bamboo and carve holes into its side to create a small flute. Lay this upon an altar to attract her blessings.

Thalia rules music in general and comedy. Stand-up comics, comedy writers, musical comedy performers, or anyone needing/wanting to improve their sense of humor should invoke Thalia. Her symbol is the comedy mask. She loves all varieties of flowers, but especially ones with long stems and clusters of fluffy, feathery plumage like blossoms that tickle such as strawberry foxglove, gay feathers, ageratum, torch lilies, butterfly bush, black knights, astilbe, snapdragons, and hyacinth. Smiling bouquets on an altar are sure to attract her attention.

Melpomene is the muse of tragedy and drama. The tragedy mask is her symbol. Melpomene can also be summoned by chopping onion until you are moved to tears. Call out her name as you taste your tears to fill your spirit with theatrical success.

Terpsichore is the muse of the dance. Star anise is used to summon Terpsichore. You must lay five whole and perfect pieces of star anise in a circle upon your altar or you can place one in each corner of a dance floor and the fifth in the center. Leave them for as long as possible. Sweep up and replace after they have been broken.

Erato incites erotic poetry, the erotic arts, and mime. Erato will be drawn to shelled and crushed cardamom seeds. Sprinkle, infuse, and season your food and beverages as often as possible. You can also place some ground cardamom in a strip of tinfoil rolled up in the shape of a bowl. Place the foil bowl upon the stove and heat until cardamom smokes and catches fire. This method arouses Erato in her most passionate form.

Polyhymnia is the muse of sacred songs. Call upon her to inspire the creation of songs or to strengthen the singing voice or for creativity in the spiritual realm. Cut a golden apple in half. Make the cut in a horizontal line through the core to reveal the five-pointed star within the apple. Insert a small piece of paper with your name and your creative desire written on it inside the center of the five-pointed star. Drizzle with honey and then replace the two halves of the apple. Tie them together with gold ribbon. Now place the apple outside under a flourishing tree. You can also eat golden apples drizzled with honey after offering Polyhymnia her share.

Urania is the muse of astronomy, of the fixed stars. I would summon her for discovery or for stardom. Plums are the sacred food of Urania, because their dark purple background with small whitish gray dots reflects the image of the night sky filled with stars. She also enjoys honey because it comes from the most sacred of the winged creatures. Place a bowl of plums drizzled with honey under a night sky and chant the name of Urania to invoke stardom or new and creative discoveries within your field.

Calliope is a heroic and poetic muse. She is the greatest of the muses, the mother of Orpheus by Apollo. Orpheus was the Thracian bard whose music charmed trees and rocks. Calliope loves to hear someone singing or chanting her name. However do not attempt this if you cannot hold a tune. Calliope means "beautiful of voice" in Greek and she is quick to aid those already blessed with strong and beautiful singing voices. She is most supportive of opera singers, stunt men and women, anyone in the field of competitive sports, and screenwriters of adventure films. She is also good for mystery writers and anyone needing a touch of eloquence in their work. Obtain some powdered spirulina at the health food store and sprinkle it out in a spiral design on your altar or table. Visualize Calliope spiraling into and opening the guarded treasure house of your creative mind. Or ask her to charm others with the melodic sound of your voice.

Iris is not a muse but the goddess of imagination herself. She is the feminine counterpart of Hermes. Iris can be summoned for any kind of inspiration. She can always be found under a rainbow and it is wise to call out her name whenever you see one to obtain her blessings of creativity. To call forth her powers at other times, prepare an offering of figs (fresh or dried) powdered with wheat germ, drizzled with honey, and sprinkled with rainbow glitter. Leave this offering outside after a rainstorm.

THE CHARIOT SPELL

INGREDIENT

horseshoe crab shell

The Chariot is the seventh card of the major arcana in the tarot. The Chariot signifies success in travel and victory and swiftness in the business of travel or any business connected with vehicles. Use this spell if you are a car salesman, chauffeur or driver, own a travel business, travel for work, or simply want success in planning a business trip or buying a car. The Chariot card is ruled by the sign of Cancer. The Crab is the symbol of this astrological sign. A horseshoe crab shell is a perfect magical talisman to summon Chariot energy. Even its name holds the magic of movement. Horses and shoes are both used to help us ride and walk our path. The horseshoe is also a symbol of good luck. The horseshoe crab is shaped like a horseshoe yet it also sports a spike or stinger at its tail. The shell is a magical talisman for both luck and serious protection and defense.

Obtain a horseshoe crab shell and place it on your altar or table. Place one of your business cards underneath the shell to protect your business and make it prosper. Imagine the plate or armor of the crab as an armor to protect your weak spots and nurture your success. If you are having problems with any aspect of your work, write the obstacles on the back of the card. Pierce the card through the center with the spike of the tail. Let the card remain there as if upon a skewer. Visualize your obstacles being punctured and defeated. Do not remove the card until you begin to see your obstacles being cut through. If you have a specific goal or plan, write it on the back of the card. Place the card under the front end of the horseshoe crab shell. Let it remain there until your goal has been accomplished.

THE EVERYTHING BAGEL SPELL

"The pursuit of knowledge for its own sake, an almost fanatical love of justice, and the desire for personal independence, these are the features of the Jewish tradition which make me thank my lucky stars I belong to it."
—*Albert Einstein*

INGREDIENTS

an everything bagel

Just last year, a fellow informed me that "the Jews are in charge of all banking and own the largest percentage of all the world's wealth." A few days later, a client of mine came for a consultation and brought along her eight-year-old daughter. While her mother was in the bathroom, the little girl asked me if I was a Jew or a witch? I told her that I considered myself Jewitch. The little girl then proceeded to inform me that witches worshipped the devil and the Jews killed Christ. When I asked her where she'd learned this, she answered "In school." Alarmed, I questioned her mother, who seemed very nonchalant about the matter.

"Oh, you know, they learn all kinds of things in school these days," was her answer. She made no effort to correct the child's erroneous beliefs.

The following week, I found myself in Berlin. I overheard a woman use a popular saying which loosely translated means "When will the Jews pay?" I suppose finding out that the term had been used in the 1920s or '30s would not have shocked me. But somehow the revelation that the expression was still in wide use in the year 2000 sent me reeling. The woman claimed it was just an old adage used to refer to a person who can constantly get away with things in business. I asked her why the Germans didn't feel that the Jews had "paid" enough. How much more could they possibly pay than with 6 million lives and all their worldly possessions? "It's just an expression," she sighed. And then without blinking an eye she continued with her response: "The Jews, my dear, must always pay. It will never be enough!"

A week later I did a live radio interview over the phone with a station in Wyoming. The interviewer wanted to know where you could obtain a certain ingredient I had mentioned in one of my spellbooks. The ingredient was Kosher salt. He asked, while on the air, if that was something *they* had poured on Jesus' wounds. He then went on to ask me if I would like to be burned at the stake, and wanted to know whether or not I practiced black magic. Mind you, this was all good-ole-boy radio humor—harmless fun, in his eyes. I found it unnerving and completely offensive. I thought, *Get a life and get an education*, but I said simply that sea salt or coarse salt would work just as well; no, I did not practice evil magic,* and that I actually preferred my steak pink or medium rare. (He deserved a different kind of response but I was unprepared to deliver it at that time.)

The following Sunday, I fell into a deep depression. I decided to turn the day around by engaging in an old family Sunday morning tradition, the everything bagel brunch. As I prepared my meal, I had a sudden insight concerning all the myths surrounding the Jewish people. There is no question that the Jewish people are extremely gifted and talented and blessed and have contributed much to the world. But many of the things still believed about them are completely preposterous. I came to the conclusion that these myths are perpetuated due to the magical properties of their Sunday morning meals.

Bagel comes from the Yiddish word *beigen* which means "to bend" or "to twist." Ha. This is the same as the meaning

---

*The term *black magic* is racially derogatory and should not be used when referring to "evil magical works." *Black magic* was a term created by the early Church Fathers to describe the ancient African religion of Voodon or Ife, meaning "Life." The implication is that magic practiced by the black race is of the devil, whereas magic practiced by the white race is "good." The truth is, I do practice black magic, as I am quite enamored of the Yoruban orishas (gods and goddesses) and several other African pantheons.

of *wicca*, the Celtic root word of "witchcraft." You might as well be saying "witch" when you say "bagel." Yes, the word itself is wrapped in magicality. It is a holy food, much holier than the doughnut, perhaps equal with the pretzel in mysticality, but has anyone ever heard of the everything pretzel? I think not!

I began to analyze the ingredients of the everything bagel. What exactly was its bend and its twist? First of all, it is a form of bread, and all breads represent money. Salt and sesame symbolize great wealth. The appearance of onion, garlic, and caraway all in one twist, is sure to produce the most enduring kind of love, a love so powerful it could not help but provoke jealousy and anger. Onion, garlic, and rye would also produce an incredible amount of protective armor, enough to help one survive the worst of misfortune and persecution. And then there is the plentiful poppy, sprinkled in such great measure that it is sure to induce the most powerful of illusions. *No wonder*, I thought, *the world thinks we control all the wealth. No wonder they are so twisted with the illusion that we are important enough to make business deals with the devil. No wonder, even after all these years, they still imagine we are the powerful slayers of the son of God.*

Yes. It all made sense. The everything bagel is high-powered Jew food. And it doesn't stop there. Think of all the things put on the everything bagel—the shmear! Why, cream cheese alone has a five-thousand-year-old reputation of being both adored and despised. Scallion and chive are considered dangerous aphrodisiacs—foods of the devil, if you will. And smoked fish is definitely a fiery derivative of the deep, dark underworld. Lox, sturgeon, whitefish, sable, caviar—all expensive powerful fish. They represent money and mystery. There is also the dreaded herring! Herring has always been one of the *cheapest* fish around. The herring or sardine is often canned in a tightly sealed "ghettoized" tin. These cheap little fish are rumored to be clannish, preferring to stick together with their own kind. (Hmmm ...) A pickle on the side is said to instigate gossip and instill rumors. Some kalamata olives on the plate scream "sagaciousness." A slice of tomato on top—why that just oozes charm. That's a lot of everything on that bagel. Plus it is eaten on a Sunday, the astrological day of fame and glory.

The everything bagel is definitely a Jewish spell. But you don't have to be Jewish to perform it. It will not make you wealthy, powerful, or wise. But it is sure to bend circumstances to create the illusion that you are all those things. Eat the everything bagel when you want to create a certain aura around yourself of well-being and prosperity. Perhaps you have a business situation in which you need people to think you are much more successful and much more wealthy than you really are, because that way they will be willing to invest their money in you. Perhaps you need to build up your reputation, make yourself look really scary and tough, like a Christ killer.

I'll tell you the secret to success in this ritual. It's all about piling stuff on. The more you can pile on the everything bagel, the more bullshit you can get people to believe about you. It's true. The only thing you should never, ever put on a bagel is *ham*. No ham. No bacon. No pork. No. No. No. This is considered sacrilegious and brings very bad luck.

It is because of the hole in the bagel that none of the materialistic magic manifests. It slips through the hole and appears only as an illusion. However the spiritual blessings the everything bagel bestows are innumerable. It is most definitely protective and should be eaten during the most dangerous of times. It can also be used to cancel out debts. (Only debts that you feel are unjustified.) Simply put the names of your creditors in the hole of the bagel and chant, *"Ikh bin im shuldik di lokh fun beygl,"* meaning, I owe him the hole in the bagel (I owe him nothing).

THE MINUTE YOU WALKED INTO THE ROOM SPELL

INGREDIENTS

whole chestnut
lime peel
honey
yellow candle
piece of gold-colored silk

This spell conjures distinction and recognition. Use it to make people sit up and take notice when you walk into a room. It is very useful for those whose business depends on social interaction. It will help create a crowd for you to work. This spell involves the making of a talisman. It must be done on a Sunday during a waxing moon phase.

Boil a whole unpeeled chestnut for six minutes in order to soften it. Remove the chestnut from the water and allow it to cool. Using a screwdriver or ice pick, drill a small hole into the chestnut. Drizzle a small amount of honey into the hole and then stuff in a small piece of lime peel. Seal the hole up by dripping the wax of a yellow candle over it. Let the chestnut stand in the sun. The chestnut can be left outside or on a windowsill. At some point during the day, the sunlight must directly hit the chestnut. At sunset wrap the chestnut in a piece of golden silk and carry as a talisman for distinction.

Chestnut, lime, and honey are all ruled by the sun. The sun establishes fame, glory, attention, and honor. Chestnuts hold the vibration of love and they also promote conversation. Limes are associated with power. Honey represents wisdom, wealth, and wonder. Honey also draws attention to whatever it is mixed with. Sealing a talisman with wax is the way to fuel your wish with divine fire. Carry this talisman to make lasting impressions.

THE ODIN SPELL

INGREDIENTS

nine alphabet blocks
some fishing line or wood glue
a doorframe

Are you a printer, Web designer, publisher, poet, sailor, or business traveler? It is the god Odin who rules all of these fields. He brings good winds to sailors, safety to the traveler, and helps all whose business is associated with the word or printed image. Odin hung upside down on the World Tree and sacrificed one of his eyes in order to receive the Runes, the sacred alphabet. This enabled him to create in the same way that the Mother Goddess created. In the Bible it states that G-d spoke the names of things and they then came into existence. This signifies the beginning of the patriarchal rule. Before this time, it was believed that the world and all things were born out of the womb of the Mother Goddess. Odin and his sacrifice changed that. From that time forward things were born out of the Word. Those in publishing, Web design, writing, even advertising and marketing, would do well to honor Odin for success in their careers. His number is nine, representing creativity, for nine is the number of months it takes to bear a child.

You will need nine alphabet blocks to perform this spell. Spell out the nine-letter word *abundance* and then verbalize specifically what it is you want abundance in. Hang these letters upside down with fishing line above the frame of a door. You can also use wood glue to paste the letters to the top of the frame. I hope you are in good shape, because you must now do a headstand within the doorframe. You may have someone assist you if necessary. While standing on your head, look up with one eye open and one eye shut. (I would never suggest that you actually put out one of your eyes. That would be *very un*lucky and *very un*abundant.) You should now be able to read the letters upright. Say "Abundance" out loud nine times and then come down out of the headstand. You have just undergone a simplified but powerful rite of Odin. The letters are now in your command. Use them wisely and prosper.

THE OLDEST PROFESSION

INGREDIENTS

blueberries
seedless green grapes
strawberries
mangoes*
mint leaves
lemon

Thanks to the prostitutes of former ages much magical lore was preserved and recorded, especially recipes and spells concerning love and money. Luckily these girls got around a lot more than the witches (or perhaps they were witches) and spread the word. I offer up this spell in gratitude to those working in the oldest profession.

Strawberries, mango, and mint combined create sexual craving. Eat them to cause others to desire you. Seedless grapes create an emphasis on recreational as opposed to procreative sex. Green grapes are eaten to attract money. Grapes and mangoes are eaten together to beat out competition and give you a financial edge. Blueberries and lemon combined create a field of protection around you and should be eaten along with taking practical measures for safety and security. Lemon and mint are used together for purification, and

---

*male prostitutes should substitute banana for mango. Transgender or cross-dressers should use both.

strawberries combined with lemon cleanse and refresh the spirit, bring cheerfulness, optimism, and increased feelings of self-worth.

Wash all fruit and mint leaves and cut into small pieces. Combine in large bowl and squeeze the juice of the lemon over the fruit salad. Mix well and eat during any moon phase. (If you eat during a waxing phase, emphasis will be on money. During a waning moon phase, the emphasis is on protection.)

While I'm on the subject of fruit salad, with just a small modification of this recipe, it becomes a protection and prosperity spell for gamblers. Substitute watermelon for mango. Watermelon and strawberry are said to make you lucky with the dice and cards. Seedless green grapes will increase your winnings. Mint, lemon, and blueberry should be eaten if you have gambling debts or to protect you from the mobsters who want to break your legs.

THE OPEN SCISSORS

Ever wonder why so many undeserving people get ahead? If ever there was a person to send the hounds after it would have been Tallyho, a selfish, uncaring weasel of a person, yet clever as a fox. Not much talent but a lot of hard sell and hardball had landed her a job in one of the top New York hair salons. She made a name for herself mostly by stealing clients from behind her co-workers' backs. She also had an incredible way of sucking up to famous models, and Tallyho's boyfriend was one of the top heroin dealers in the city, which was another reason why the models flocked to Tallyho's chair. They could get cut and colored and shot up all in one stop. Tallyho was also very underhanded. If she saw someone coming through the salon who looked like they had even a shred of talent, Tallyho would cut them off at the pass. She liked to be surrounded by the most untalented stylists because they made her look good.

Polly, a most talented stylist, had worked six years as a shampoo girl before getting her own chair, but unfortunately the chair she was given was right next to Tallyho's. Polly watched in amazement as Tallyho popped her gum, spit in clients' faces, and prattled on in a loudmouthed, low-class offensive drawl worse than that of Eliza Doolittle. Tallyho's breath always smelled of booze from the night before and early that morning. Polly watched as Tallyho sloppily dropped globs of color down the faces of her clients, staining their cheeks. Often she made mistakes and clumps of hair would fall out of her clients' heads. Many mistakes were made but most of the models were too high to notice it. And if they did, Tallyho would threaten to cut off their drug supplies if they dared to complain. Yes, no matter how offensive Tallyho was, the woman continued to climb up Rapunzel's ladder to success.

Unbelievable, thought Polly.

Tallyho had also done everything in her power to make Polly look bad, feel unwelcome, and never rise from the position of lowly shampoo girl. Now that Polly had finally gotten her own chair, Tallyho was madder than hell. At least once a week Tallyho would sharply turn to Polly with a pair of open scissors in her hand. With a maniacal grin

Tallyho would croak, "Watch out, sweetie, or you'll fall into my open scissors. Snip, snip, snip," threatened Tallyho while cutting the air with her sharp scissors, dangerously close to Polly's face. It was Tallyho's way of saying, "You'll be cut to shreds if you cross me." Apparently this threat had kept most in the salon in their place, but Polly decided to put Tallyho in her own wicked place. One night on a full moon, Polly stayed late in the salon. She took a pair of sharp shears and inserted a paper with Tallyho's signature in the shears. She cut sharply through the paper, cutting Tallyho's name in half. Polly spoke these words while cutting:

"Into the open scissors you go,
all your power and control cut low.
And all that you reap, so shall you sow.
Everything you give returns to you,
all you cut off is cut off from you
as the open scissors cut you through."

Polly repeated the chant nine times and cut Tallyho's name to shreds.

On the next full moon Polly was working on her client and minding her own business. It seemed Tallyho was having a bad hair day. Her top client was most dissatisfied. Not only was the 'do horrible but Tallyho's boyfriend had never shown up to deliver the drugs. The hair diva was pissed. She was not used to apologizing or sucking up to people. Just then her cell phone rang. It seemed Tallyho's class-A boyfriend had landed himself in jail by selling smack to undercover cops. Tallyho hit the roof and demanded to take a break (even though she had four clients waiting) to go and bail him out.

She stormed out of the salon and hailed a cab. She actually stole the cab out from under a little old lady who had been waiting for over seven minutes. Tallyho jumped in the stolen cab and barked an address to the cabbie. When the recording of Judge Judy came on to tell Tallyho to fasten her seat belt, Tallyho spat forth "F— you, Judge Judy! I hate those f'ing recordings," she wailed at the cabbie. The loud, maniacal, annoying, and horrible-sounding voice of Tallyho caught the cabbie off guard and he slammed into the Lubavitch Mitzvah Mobile (a special van that drives around New York to perform good deeds) in front of him. It was a hard hit but luckily no one was hurt. Because everyone was wearing their seat belts. Except for Tallyho, that is. She broke her hand in eighteen places and I don't imagine she will ever be able to steadily hold a pair of scissors again.

Nope, she can't cut hair anymore, and her boyfriend dumped her because she could no longer help him fasten his little Ziploc dope bags. I don't think she can even press all the touch-tone keys needed to collect unemployment over the phone. No, she will most definitely have to go down there in person and bitch while she waits in long long lines. Only thing is, she can't really collect unemployment because she was working with a stolen green card. Guess the diva Tallyho will just have to go back to wherever she came from and spread the joy around.

In the meanwhile, Polly is now managing the salon in New York. Business is thriving. All the talented shampoo girls have chairs and most of the top models are in drug rehab.

THE POSERS

INGREDIENTS

raw onion

The posers are wannabes, people who pose as something they are not. Usually they attach to and ingratiate themselves with people who they are envious of. Also the posers pose themselves in position. They wait until they find a vulnerable or weak spot and then they step in and take over at playing what they had been practicing and lying about being for years.

If you feel you have a poser attached to you, here is what to do. The onion with its layers can be used to peel away and uncover deception. Simply carve the name of the assumed poser on the outside of an onion. Then begin to peel away all the layers until there is nothing left. Leave all the layers of skin out in the sun. Expose them to the elements on a windowsill or on a front porch. If the person in question is a poser, he or she will be exposed.

A note: Do not expect immediate results or exposure in a rational way. For example, an exposé in the news may not occur. Your boss may not confront and expose the lies of the poser. But in some way, the poser will be revealed. Here is a true example: A woman was posing as a powerful hereditary witch. She would hang around the occult shops and brag about certain spells she cast to cause the downfall of others. She claimed to have knowledge and power of all occult arts handed down to her from her family. What the real truth is we may never know. However, it is interesting to note that each time this woman bragged of another powerful exploit that supposedly resulted in causing someone's demise, one of her teeth would either fall out or rot in her mouth. Her bad magic became manifest in her mouth. Anyone looking at her could clearly see that the negativity she generated fell only upon herself. Even more interesting is that this woman claimed to be an adept of a very powerful form of evil sorcery known as Saturnian magic. Saturn is the ruler of teeth!

THE RED FOODS

INGREDIENTS

red apple
beets
red cabbage
red onions
red peppers
red radish

Nanette was just a girl who couldn't say no. Someone once told her to say yes to life and she just couldn't stop. Three years of psychotherapy and even eight sessions of hypnotherapy couldn't teach Nanette to say no. She said yes to every party and event that her friends and acquaintances invited her to. She was out every night saying yes to someone or something. She got very little sleep and it got so bad that she lost her job because she was late to work once too often. Not only that, she lost all her friends, too, because Nanette accepted *every* invitation and it was impossible for her to be in three or four places at the same time. People got tired of her irresponsibility. She also maxed out all her credit cards from buying all kinds of ridiculous things offered to her through mail, phone, television, and Internet ads. Finally, desperate not to lose another job, Nanette came to see me.

This was my remedy, and apparently it worked. These red foods must be chopped and diced, mixed together, and eaten on a Tuesday. The color red is like a stop sign. It can be used magically to bring something to a halt. Tuesday is the day of Mars. Mars energy can be used for any kind of battles. Apple is to promote self-love and self-respect. Beets are ruled by Saturn, also known as the planet of negativity. Nanette needed all the negative energy she could get. Saturn is also the planet of restriction and discipline. I told Nanette to boil small beets for eight or nine minutes before peeling and slicing. It was important for the beets to remain crisp and firm. Nanette needed some willpower. She sure had been acting crazy. In ancient Greece, eating red cabbage was believed to cure insanity. All head vegetables were believed to represent and influence the head or mind. The red cabbage should be sliced and then steamed in a pan, the idea being first to open the mind, and then to apply some heat to change the thinking patterns. Red onions, peppers, and radish are all used for protection and self-defense. Nanette needed to take care of herself. These three reds should be added and eaten raw to retain all their protective powers.

After eating these red foods for three Tuesdays in a row,

Nanette began to say no. She got so worked up by the spell that when the phone rang, Nanette just picked it up and yelled no into the receiver. Luckily it was an annoying sales-person. Still Nanette couldn't stop. She no'd herself through the entire week and month. It was terrific. She got a lot of work done and ended up getting a promotion and raise at her new job. The company loved No No Nanette. She was good for business with her new no-nonsense attitude. She was able to clear up her credit card debt with the increase in salary, and she says her life is shaping up. Her friends are once again beginning to respect her. Whenever she feels her no slipping away, Nanette prepares a booster dose of the reds.

Note: I told Nanette she could season her reds with a dash of olive oil, vinegar, salt, pepper, and sugar. Olive oil and salt will promote the longevity of her new habits. Vin-egar and pepper are sacred to both Mars and Saturn. They increase discipline. Sugar sweetens the sound of her no.

THE THINKING CAP

INGREDIENTS

two shower caps
assortment of sesame, poppy, and sunflower
seeds

The Thinking Cap is a tool for students, researchers, or writers. It can be used by anyone in need of a creative brain-storm. What you need essentially is a bain-marie for the brain. This allows you to cook up your ideas evenly and not suffer from mental burnout.

You will need one tight-fitting bathing or shower cap and one looser-fitting one. Place the tighter one over your head. Fill the looser one with an assortment of sesame, poppy, and sunflower seeds. Then place it over the tight-fitting cap already on your head. Leave this cap of inspiration on for at least twenty minutes. Remain active during this time. Walk around or create some kind of movement. Shake your head often to season it with ideas. Chant:

> *"Open, sesame, open, sunflower,*
> *unlock/reveal my creative power.*
> *Now open, poppy, let me dream,*
> *imagine things I've never seen.*
> *Shake me loose from clouds and fears,*
> *seed my brain with good ideas."*

Think of your brain as a fertile womb being seeded or impregnated with ideas. After a minimum of twenty minutes remove the cap and lie down for five minutes. Then begin your work.

THREE-PEPPER PASTA FOR PROTECTION AND SUCCESS

INGREDIENTS

bell peppers (green, orange, red)
olive oil

garlic cloves
onion (yellow or white)
fresh parsley
paprika
salt and pepper
cherry or grape tomatoes
pasta

This delicious and nutritious dish is considered a success and protection formula. All bell peppers are considered foods of protection. However the colors contain their own properties. Red is for energy (or love), orange for success, and green for money. So by eating the tricolor peppers, we can protect our assets, our career path, and our energy. Parsley is mercurial and opens channels for success, yet it is also said to drive away evil. Salt brings prosperity and black pepper gives a commanding presence. Yet both are also used for protection. Olive oil is used for prosperity and lends long life and health. It can be used to maintain our blessings. Garlic and onion ward off evil and increase stamina. Paprika and tomatoes are mostly used for love, but combined they increase self-love, self-respect, and self-confidence. Pasta is a mercurial food and is eaten to inspire creativity.

This pasta can be eaten to protect your career in addition to promoting it. It can be eaten when you feel your success is threatened in any way. A great recipe to prepare after receiving any kind of promotion. It will protect you from any jealousy over your success and help strengthen you to meet your new responsibilities successfully. The formula is also good for anyone who is working too hard since it prevents creative or physical burnout. Prepare and eat this any time you feel your job is threatened by disruptive forces (whether those forces are internal or external.)

Coat a pan with olive oil and heat. For magical purposes it is best to cook with cast iron. It adds more power and protection to the spell. Add finely chopped garlic (two cloves) and half an onion. Add eight sprigs of fresh parsley with stems removed. Add long thin strips of sliced green, orange, and red pepper. (Use the equivalent of two whole peppers in all. Choose the color you want to emphasize for the whole pepper and use a half of the other two colors.) Season with paprika, salt, and pepper. Add twenty cherry or grape tomatoes sliced in half. Cover and steam for ten to sixteen minutes. Cook pasta separately. Combine and eat. You can add Parmesan or Romano cheese to include a nurturing aspect.

Note: There may be side effects to this spell. Since several of the ingredients have properties of love, (sometimes even peppers are used for love) it may cause a love affair to begin at work. This is rare, but can occur. I find that in most cases, it works by increasing your own feelings of self-esteem and promotes the love and respect of others in your field.

TMI SPELLS

The following two spells are designed to combat TMI (too much information). The first is to assist in eliminating useless information and to help you quickly sift through it all and find what you need. The second is used to create more space in your system to absorb new information.

I. MINOS AND THE LABYRINTH OF INFORMATION

INGREDIENTS

aloe plant
ginger
vanilla
brick dust

I see you are lost in the labyrinth of useless information as you surf the Net. You must appease the sacred Minotaur, guardian of the labyrinth, otherwise you will get eaten alive like the Athenian youths. I suggest aloe, the sacred plant of the Cretan bull god. Aloe is a magical prescription to summon the Minotaur to guide you safely through the tangles of the Web. Keep a large aloe plant next to your computer. Cut open a leaf and massage the aloe into the fingers of both hands before you log on. Aloe is also calming and soothing. The plant will improve your patience and ability to absorb information.

I see that your collection of useless information is not limited to the Internet. Oh, no, countless hours are wasted on phone calls, faxes, interviews, and power lunches that merely circle you round to where you started from. As you search to make the right connections, you need to find the shortest distance between two points. Master powder will help you develop a straight line of connection and more quickly attract the information you need. Master powder can be made by combining powdered ginger, powdered vanilla bean, and red brick dust. Use a knife to scrape the side of a brick. Collect the dust and add it to a finely ground vanilla bean and powdered gingerroot. Dust your hands daily for more direct, meaningful and to-the-point interactions. Use it daily until you have all the contacts and information you need.

II. TO IMPROVE THE MEMORY AND LEARNING SKILLS

INGREDIENTS

sage
cucumber
lavender
basil
lemon
coconut
cinnamon

This spell is to assist in the assimilation and memorization of new information. My Spanish teacher once told me; the older you get, the slower you get, from the top of the head to the bottom of the toes. To a certain extent this is true. We must deal with the reality of aging. But on another level, we think or absorb more slowly because we are carrying a lot more weight or information. What do you do if a ship is too heavy? You begin to throw the less vital things over-board. What are you carrying around that is outdated and no good? Get rid of it!

The mind of a child is very facile. It's like a vacuum sucking up knowledge at an accelerated pace. The mind of an adult is more bogged down. The vacuum bag is full, which makes the suction capacity low. Our heads become overfilled and it is difficult to take in any more when your head is full.

We must empty our bags (brains) to increase the rate of

our learning capacity. It can be done. It is not impossible. The combination of sage, cucumber, lavender, basil, lemon, and coconut is a traditional witches' brew to clear and bless a space. In this case, the space will be our heads. It has also been proven that the eyes, tongue, hands, and arms are connected with memory and absorption of information as well. This is why we learn and memorize best by writing, reading, and speaking. So we are going to prepare a mixture and cleanse and empty the hands and arms, leading up to the head, focusing as well on the eyes, ears, and tongue.

Obtain a coconut with its milk. Cut the coconut in half so that you have a bowl. Fill this bowl with the milk of the coconut. Add lemon juice, lavender flowers, cucumber slices, rubbed sage, and freshly chopped basil. Let the mixture sit for about an hour. Then slowly dip your hands into the bowl. With your right hand, hold the fingers of your left hand. Massage the left hand, moving all the way up the left arm. Massage under the armpit and then behind the left shoulder blade and up the back of the neck. Do the same to the right hand using your left hand. Using both hands, after dipping your fingers in the liquid in the bowl, begin at the back of the neck and move the hands up and over the head. Run them down along the face, making sure to touch the closed eyes, the lips, tongue, and teeth, and then spread the hands out over the ears. Repeat this procedure three times.

For most effective results, stand in shower and end by bending the head down and dumping the whole bowl over the head. This part of the ritual will cleanse your mind and clear away all obstacles that stand in the way of you absorbing new information.

Now that the mind is clear, you need to create a vacuum effect to suck in the new information quickly. Obtain a yellow legal pad and, using key words or phrases, write down what kind of information you need to learn. Using your fingers, rub some cinnamon powder over these words and then hold the paper over your head and visualize the words you have written. Cinnamon is said to have incredible drawing power (like a vacuum). It also brings swift success. Repeat this ritual any time you feel resistance to learning.

TO COLLECT DEBTS

INGREDIENTS
clove chewing gum
cork
corkscrew
walnuts
nutcracker

I. This spell is for professional bill collectors or anyone needing success in collecting monies owed. Begin by chewing a piece of clove gum on a new moon. Crack the gum hard and firmly grind into it with your teeth. Visualize the person or company who owes you money feeling compelled to pay you. Clove is a spice of control. Gum is actually used in magical formulas to clear paths and remove obstacles. After ten minutes spit the gum out hard. See how far you can spit it. (I suggest you do this outside.) The farther you throw it, the farther your influence will reach. After you spit the gum, call out the amount of money owed to you. Clap your hands together three times and then put them in your pockets or touch your purse. The clapping of hands is a way to send out spirits to do their work. To end by touching the purse or pockets is a way to let the spirits know where you want this sum of money to land. Wait at least two weeks until the full moon for results. If you have not obtained your money move on to phase II of the spell.

II. On the full moon, write the name of the person or company that owes you money down the side of a cork from a wine bottle. Twist a corkscrew all the way down into the cork and imagine turning the screws on the ones who owe you money. Visualize them reaching deep in their pockets to pay you. Leave the corkscrew embedded in the cork for two weeks until the new moon. On the new moon, slowly twist the corkscrew out of the cork while calling out the sum of money owed you. Chew a piece of clove gum and after it's nice and soft, take it out of your mouth and press it onto the top of the cork. Hold this cork in the right hand and squeeze hard several times a day for another thirteen days. Visualize yourself receiving the money. Cork is used to contain and hold energy. The spiral shape of the corkscrew is one of the most powerful symbols a witch can use to send energy. If you still have not received payment, move to phase III of this spell.

III. On the dark moon (which occurs one day before the new moon) sit at a table and shell as many walnuts as you can using a nutcracker. Visualize on each nut the face or name of the person or company who owes you money. As you pull out the flesh of the nut, visualize pulling the money owed you out of this person or company. As you crack each nut, visualize yourself removing the obstacles, cracking through the veneer, and penetrating the walls of avoidance. Do not stop cracking until you have clearly visualized every single obstacle in your way being overcome and the money securely in your hands. At this point, chew a piece of clove gum and hold the visualization for as long as you can, and then let it go completely as you spit the gum into the pile of cracked nuts. Clap your hands three times and then touch your pockets or purse. Walnuts are symbolic of the head and can be used to influence or plant commands in the mind. Walnuts were also once used as monetary exchange and therefore represent payment or salary.

I advise you to work these spells along with *real* phone calls, faxes, E-mails, or good old-fashioned letters from your lawyers to collect these monies. I have used these spells many times with much success. I usually never have to move beyond phase I. There was one exception, however. It took me almost nine months to collect monies owed me from a certain magazine I wrote an article for. I understand I am not the only writer to suffer this abuse. Apparently magazines are notorious for not paying writers, and I believe that in some way they are impervious to magic. I finally received payment after parking myself on the couch of the reception area. I sat there cracking nuts and refused to leave without my check!

TO EXECUTE PLANS

INGREDIENTS

lime
bay
allspice
cinnamon
clove
a red brick
red rose petals

This recipe uses traditional witches' ingredients associated with power and success. The combination of lime, allspice, and clove is used to initiate action. Bay and cinnamon bring expansion. Red rose along with cinnamon will open channels of cooperation among people. Brick is made by firing clay and represents the element of earth (materialization) and fire (actualization). Bricks also symbolize building and paving the way. Use this talisman to help implement plans. It is also a great talisman for all executives and administrators.

Place a red brick on an altar or desk and surround it with a circle of crushed bay leaves, powdered allspice, cinnamon, clove, and crushed red rose petals. Lift the brick and use it as a paperweight to hold down any plans you are trying to execute or set into motion. Do not remove it until the project is successfully off the ground. This spell is also recommended for architects or those in the construction business.

TO FIND A LOST OBJECT

*It doesn't belong to my grandmother, she just used it when
necessary. She used to sit at the kitchen table with her
cigarette and laugh her ass off about the whole thing. She
was very serious about the whole thing, but could not
avoid the humor of poor Poncio running around with his
balls in a knot, after her lost little items.*
——Juan Pablo Vicente

INGREDIENTS
a dish towel in the kitchen

This spell was given to me by my dear friend Juan Pablo.
It was taught to him by his grandmother Angela Sosa. It
was taught to me one night during an *asado* (barbecue)
at my house. Someone had heated water for the maté[1] and
afterward the little top to my teakettle had disappeared.
This teakettle is very special to me. It is quite unique,
an antique, and it was a gift from my dearly beloved
brother, the last gift he gave me before he died. It was a
most precious and irreplaceable item. Of course we looked
in all the normal places—not to be found. My dear friend
La Bicha (not a dearer friend to be found) even went
through two large bags of trash. No luck. There were four
of us bug-eyed and tired (it was going on 6:00 A.M.),

---

[1] a special Argentine beverage made with yerba maté herb and drunk out of a gourd.

roaming around the kitchen and living room like imbeciles looking and looking in all the places we had already looked before.

I was surprised the search even went on that long. Friends of former years would have wished me luck or told me to let it go as they headed out the door to go home to bed. Not these Argentines. They don't give up. They don't let go. Honestly, it was getting ridiculous. All of a sudden, Juan Pablo seemed to fly into a demonic and sadistic rage. He grabbed a dish towel and tied it into a fierce knot. He bellowed out in a commanding voice:

> *"Poncio Pilatos, Las bolas te ato.*
> *Si aparece, bien,*
> *si no, nunca mas te las desato!"*

I was very shocked. I had no idea what was going on. I thought he'd lost his mind.

"Okay, c'mon. Let's stop looking. Sit down and smoke a cigarette. Give him time to do his work. If we continue to move stuff around it might confuse him or make him angry. Let's just leave it alone for a while. Let Poncio do his work. He'll find it for us. He doesn't like his balls tied up in knots," said Juan Pablo matter-of-factly as he sat down by the fire and lit a smoke.

"Yes, okay," I said, and sat down to join him. I guess I am perfectly used to my friends losing their minds. La Bicha and Tomas also stopped looking and took a smoke break. It was then that Juan Pablo explained to me that this was an old spell to find a lost object. You take a dish towel and you tie it in a knot. You say:

"Pontius Pilate, your balls I tie.
If it shows up, fine,
But if not, I'll never untie!"

You *do not* untie this knot in the dishtowel until the lost object has been found, *no matter how long it takes!*

Well, I was very intrigued by this spell, but I still thought that they would be going home now and I would be left with a knotted dish towel hanging in my kitchen till kingdom come. Not the case. Juan Pablo began to reflect as he ground out his cigarette butt.

"Lexa, where was it that you wrapped the meat?" he asked.

"Why, I wrapped it on the butcher-block counter," I answered.

"Yes, and that is the last place that the kettle top was seen," he said while jumping up and running to the freezer. Juan Pablo began to feel all the packages of wrapped meat in the freezer. He pulled out a package of skirt steaks rolled in tinfoil with a twinkle in his eye. You could feel and see the distinct shape of the kettle lid underneath the foil wrap. When I had spread out the foil to wrap the meat, the lid had gotten caught up with the package. Juan Pablo unwrapped the foil, freeing the lid and placed it lovingly back on the kettle. With a mischievous grin and a devilish laugh, he untied the knot in the dish towel, and said, "Thank you, Poncio."

Now, this may seem like nada—no magic—to you. But it was quite magical to me. First of all, I often have leftover meat at *asados*. We always buy too much. And often I have thrown away packages of frozen meat if too much time goes by before the next *asado*. It is quite possible that I may have come across the lid a few weeks later while defrosting the meat. But it is just as likely that I may have carelessly gathered up the tinfoil and thrown it away. It is also possible that the delicate Bakelite lid may have cracked from being frozen for so long.

All in all, I would say Poncio did a wonderful job, and I am now a firm believer that if you tie up his balls, he will find most anything. (My friend Loreena used this to find a pair of Jean Paul Gaultier sunglasses that she had left in a taxi cab. She also forgot to get the receipt from this cab ride. Sunglasses are almost an impossible thing to recover.[2])

Traditionally it is St. Jude who is petitioned to find lost items. But Jude is a saint and must be treated with respect. Oftentimes we are very angry and frustrated when we lose our important little things and we can't very well start mouthing off to St. Jude. The idea of tying up a saint's balls in knots is unthinkable, a sacrilege. But Pontius Pilate, on the other hand, is a perfect person to help us blow off steam. To get his balls tied up until he locates the little important things that we've misplaced in life is the perfect occupation for his lost and tortured soul. Why, he was the biggest anti-Semite of the ancient world. Don't you remem-

---

[2] I use this example to let you know that the item does not have to be something you lost in the kitchen. You may have lost it anywhere. However, I feel that the dish towel must be knotted with the chant while you are in your kitchen. And it must be kept there until the item is recovered. The kitchen is the place where women like Angela Sosa performed their powerful folk magic, and we should uphold that tradition with honor and respect.

ber him from that episode of *To Tell the Truth?* He was the one who got all the way up from his chair when Bud Collyer asked, "Will the real Christ killer please stand up?" I don't think he was particularly kind to women or witches either. He was a bad Roman magistrate, a horrible greedy politician. I can't think of any kind words that anyone ever said about Pontius Pilate. And if anyone is crying for him in Argentina, I can assure you it's only over a knotted dish towel.

TO GET A RAISE

INGREDIENTS

three cups wheat flour
two packs quick rising yeast
one teaspoon salt
two cups nonfat milk
crushed walnuts
sesame seeds
sunflower seeds
rye flour
olive oil
yellow cornmeal
large egg

The best magic for a raise in salary is to bake bread. This should be done twenty-four hours after a new moon for best results. Bread symbolizes money. You will want to use a quick-rising yeast so that it won't take forever to increase your dough.

Begin with a large mixing bowl. Add three cups wheat flour, two packages of yeast, and a teaspoon of salt. Salt and wheat also symbolize money. Mix in two cups of warm nonfat (you can never be too rich or too thin) milk to be sure you get the nurturing you need.

Beat for five minutes with an electric mixer or ten minutes by hand until the batter is elastic. Visualize your boss being flexible and maybe even bending over backward to meet your demands. Mix in one tablespoon each of crushed walnuts for salary, sesame and sunflower seeds for abundance.

Stir in a cup of rye flour with a wooden spoon. Friendly spirits live in wood, and rye will bring you the admiration, appreciation, and respect you deserve. Sprinkle another half cup of rye flour on the kneading board. (You can never be appreciated or needed enough!)

Scrape the batter on the board and begin to turn and roll in the rye. Add more appreciation (I mean rye flour) as needed. Knead briskly (but not brusquely) for about thirteen minutes (a full lunar year). The dough should be elastic and somewhat dry.

Add a tablespoon of oil (I suggest olive, for it represents success and longevity and can help you build toward your long-term financial future) to the mixing bowl. Put your dough back in and oil all sides. Cover with a warm, wet green towel and leave in a warm place for forty minutes to rise. Take this time to relax, drink a green tea, and visualize your raise in salary.

Punch the dough down and knead it gently after it has risen. Imagine the tough lines and/or gentle cajoling you will use on your boss to get him or her to agree to your raise.

Cut the dough in half. You are going to make two round loaves. One will be eaten by you. The other will be placed outside under a strong and healthy tree with many green leaves as an offering for the Goddess. (I know that money doesn't grow on trees, but if you leave the bread there, She will surely get your message and lend Her hand to your request.)

Preheat your oven to 375 degrees. Start heatin' things up. Grease two baking sheets and sprinkle a thin, even layer of cornmeal on each. There is nothing like cornmeal to summon wealth. Each piece of dough should be rolled into a ball. The round shape represents the circle of the Goddess. Roundness also removes obstacles and represents smooth sailing (or smooth baking as it were).

Cover with your green towels and allow to rise again for twenty-five minutes. (Maybe you should send a memo to your boss during this time.) The loaves may flatten at this point, but they will also spread. (Mention in that memo that you want some of that wealth spread around your way!)

Glaze the loaves now. Beat an egg with a tablespoon of water. (Eggs bring new beginnings) Brush the loaves with the mixture and sprinkle sunflower seeds, sesame seeds, and crushed walnuts or oats generously over the tops. Bake for forty minutes. During this time you should visualize your raise a done deal. Cool and eat the bread warm.

Shooting for a really big raise? A major increase in salary? Bake this bread on a full moon.

Note: Baking guideline for recipe provided by *Bake Your Own Bread* by Floss and Stan Dworkin, Plume, 1987.

TO GUARD AGAINST THEFT

INGREDIENTS

paper
three match heads
coarse salt
ground red pepper
strongbox and key

Are you tired of your ideas being stolen? Or employees, bosses, or co-workers ripping you off? Here is a powerful spell to guard against theft. Using a piece of parchment paper or heavy construction paper, draw a square. Within the square, draw a circle. Within the circle, draw a triangle. Write within the triangle whatever it is you want to protect from thieves. This symbol is an old witches' glyph or veve for protection of goods. Lay the paper in a small strongbox. Grind three match heads to a fine powder using a mortar and pestle. Add coarse salt and red pepper to the ground match heads. This is a traditional witches' formula known as Keep-Away Powder. Sprinkle the powder inside the box on top of the paper and lock with the key. Keep the key around your neck until you feel the items or ideas are no longer in danger of being stolen.

TO OPEN DOORS

INGREDIENTS

a brass doorknob
coconut milk
almond oil
pure lemon extract
two magnets

If you recall, Aunt Clara on *Bewitched* used to collect doorknobs. They are very magical, but you will only need one. It should be brass, which is a copper alloy and contains the magical properties of persuasion. I suggest looking in the hardware store or flea market for your doorknob. Once obtained, grease it with a mixture of almond oil, pure lemon extract, and coconut milk. These three ingredients are sacred to two particular spirits of the Moon and Mercury who are called upon to remove restrictions and open passages. By rubbing this potion on your doorknob, you will attract the attention and help of these spirits. If you know which door you want to open, (perhaps it is the door of a particular casting agent you've been trying to get in to see), then write the name of that person or company on a small piece of paper. Place the paper on top of the doorknob and put one of the magnets there to hold it in place. Write your name on a piece of paper and hold it in place on the other side of the doorknob with the second magnet. Chant:

> *"Spirit, please unlock the door,*
> *throw it open with a roar.*
> *Draw (name) and me very near,*
> *help to make the passage clear.*
> *By your power let us meet,*
> *by my will obtain this feat."*

If you do not know exactly which door needs to be opened, then do not use the magnets. Simply polish, rub, and turn the doorknob with the potion as you chant:

> *"Spirit, please unlock the door,*
> *throw it open with a roar.*
> *Help me on my way to steer,*
> *make my path direct and clear.*

Let no door be closed to me.
As I will, so mote it be."

This spell is best performed on Mondays or Wednesdays. Any moon phase is appropriate.

TO REGAIN A POSITION, OR, THREE SPELLS FOR WHEN YOU GET CANNED

INGREDIENTS

I.
small mirror

II.
old-fashioned scale
red candle

III.
lavender
cinnamon
ginger
vanilla extract or bean
brick dust

There are many different magical paths to travel after you have been fired from a job. Of course, the most common response would be to "go postal" with your magic. It is a normal response to want revenge or justice when someone has treated you unfairly at the workplace. Also, being fired or losing a job creates fear and insecurity about your financial future. Often anger, even unrealistic anger, surfaces in such situations. Getting revenge is not the high road, however, mostly because in order to get revenge you must use, and actually sap yourself of, vital energy in order to effectively actualize this magic. In such a time or situation, all your vital energy is probably needed to heal, regroup, and find another, better job. However, if you feel the irresistible need to strike back, here are some magical options.

I. The most effective spell, the one that will take the least of your energy, is known as the mirroring technique. You simply employ the magical reflective powers of the mirror to send back the negative energy that was sent to you. This type of work involves very little of your own vital energy being used. Simply place a small hand mirror in front of a picture of your ex-boss or superior, or you can write the name of this person and the name of the company on a small piece of paper. To use the letterhead of the business or an actual signature is even more effective. Place this in front of a mirror, or you might want to tape the paper or photo to the mirror as well. Chant:

> *"Return, return, energy burn.*
> *What you have sent me, I return.*
> *May it burn and return to you."*

Repeat this chant for nine days.

II. For justice, you will need an old-fashioned scale with trays and little weights. Place the name of offending party on one end of scale. Place yourself on the other end. Burn a red candle in the center and ask Maat the Egyptian goddess of justice to weigh the matter and bring you justice. Please be prepared to wait a full moon cycle (twenty-eight days) for results.

III. There is a special spirit who can be summoned to regain a position that has been taken. Nebiros (or Naberius) is one of the light spirits listed in *The Goetia: The Lesser Key of Solomon the King*,* a book of medieval ceremonial magic. Use lavender, cinnamon, ginger, vanilla extract or bean, and brick dust to attract the attention of this spirit. Mix all ingredients in a bowl and then sprinkle in a circle around an altar or table. In the center of this circle place a piece of paper with your name written on it and the title or job or position you wish to regain. Call to Naberius twenty-four times (his number) in a hoarse voice. Ask him to restore your position. Visualize a black crane flying above your head. This is the totem of the spirit. Leave the powder on the altar for twenty-four hours and then gather it in a pouch and wear it on your person. Allow at least twenty-four days for this magic to take effect.

---

*The Goetia: The Lesser Key of Solomon the King, translated by Samuel Liddell MacGregor Mathers, edited by Aleister Crowley, Samuel Weiser, Inc., York Beach, ME. 1995.

TO TELL THE TRUTH SPELL

INGREDIENTS

mint

rose

nutmeg

This is an old witches' brew used to get someone to tell the truth. Rub the powdered mixture into the hands and touch the person you feel is lying. They will be made to tell the truth. If you are not dealing with this person directly, I suggest you dust your hands before contacting him or her through phone, fax, or E-mail. After dusting your own hands, immerse a piece of paper with the name of this individual, or a photo, in a bowl of the mixture.

This potion can also be modified to work in specific situations. For example, if you are using this formula to obtain information about someone you plan to hire to take care of your children, please add flax seeds. Flax seeds are extremely protective toward children and are said to greatly increase your psychic awareness and ability. The combination of flax and nutmeg will bring hidden information up to the surface immediately. If your potential au pair has any skeletons in her or his closet, you'll find out pronto! Rose makes the interaction more friendly while mint makes it fast and to the point.

For investment truths add bay. Bay is used to protect financial interests and is also said to promote the truth by jarring the memory. This is a very good ingredient when lies involve the omission of key information. It is said that when bay is carried on the left side, it stops the negative interference of others in your life. Add bay to the three main ingredients and carry in a pouch on your left side to stop lies involving defamation of character or reputation.

Red pepper confuses liars. Add this to the main mixture to catch a chronic liar in his or her tracks. Also use this to pin down anyone who is making you run in circles to collect payment or work that they owe you.

Mustard is said to increase faithfulness. Add mustard if you want to find out if someone is cheating on you or stealing from you.

TRIPLE DRAW SPELL

INGREDIENTS

maple syrup
honey
molasses
cinnamon powder

The Triple Draw spell is used to draw money to a business. Lay your business card on a tinfoil sheet. Drizzle a teaspoon each of maple syrup, honey, and molasses over the card. The combination of these three is known as the triple thick. It is used to draw prosperity and make it stick. Sprinkle cinnamon powder on top of the triple thick to increase the drawing power. Fold up the business card in the tinfoil square and place in a zipper lock plastic bag. Keep in the cash register or under the doormat at the entrance of the business. If you do not use an office or one primary physical space to conduct business, carry the talisman in your wallet or briefcase.

WALL STREET SPELL

INGREDIENTS

cinnamon
clove
ginger
lemon
orange peel

Legend has it that King Solomon was taught much of the magical arts by the Queen of Sheba. According to 1 Kings 10 she paid him a mysterious visit with a caravan of camels carrying gold and spices. His wealth only increased after her arrival. *The Goetia: The Lesser Key of Solomon the King* is alleged to be a book of magic written by King Solomon. It contains a host of spirits light and dark who can be summoned to achieve various magical aims.

The light spirit Aimee is said to reveal hidden wealth and fortune. Aimee is quite fond of cinnamon, clove, ginger, lemon, and orange peel. Sprinkle a mixture of these spices on top of the great seal or pyramid on the U.S. dollar bill. Fold up the bill with the spices inside and tie it up with a gold ribbon. Place this gift on your money altar, desk, or on top of your stock portfolio. Every day from the new moon to the full moon chant:

> *"Aimee, bring wealth to me.*
> *As I will so mote it be.*
> *Lemon, clear the path,*
> *clove, do the math,*
> *ginger, lend great speed,*
> *orange, my fortune seed,*
> *cinnamon, summon swift the luck,*
> *pyramid multiply the buck.*
> *Aimee, I offer all unto thee.*
> *Bring me great wealth.*
> *So mote it be."*

Hold the wrapped dollar in your open left palm as you chant. Keep the right palm open as well and visualize Aimee giving you a gift in your empty palm. I know many investors who have prospered by invoking the spirit of Aimee.

Small bits of cinnamon bark, clove buds, crystallized orange or lemon peel, and ginger can also be chewed while chanting to Aimee. Listen carefully for information on how to uncover hidden wealth and treasure. Then begin your trading.

Like Solomon, this spirit possesses wisdom, insight, and wealth. Although not traditionally a spirit of luck, if you are a professional gambler Aimee may be beneficial to your work.

WEB DESIGNER
DOMINATRIX SPELL

INGREDIENTS

pot of soil
hair from the head of a menstruating woman
powdered dried rosebuds
gingerroot powder
sweet basil
clove
cinnamon
vanilla
mint
gold sparkles

Over three hundred persons in the field of Web and software design and computer graphics expressed exactly the same sentiments to me. They all felt capable of murder when dealing with competition and problems on the Web. Their aggressive tendencies came right to the surface and they seemed to show no shame in requesting a spell that could help them to kill hackers, competitors, viruses, system glitches, and technicalities that interfered with their work. Over half of those I spoke with requested some very old, monstrous magic. They felt that the only kind of magic to deal with the New Age technology would have to be something terrible and old.

It is in light of this information that I offer up the spell to create the basilisk or cockatrice to guard and protect your Internet files. Originally mentioned by the Biblical prophet Isaiah, the basilisk dates back to the prebiblical period. Until the eighteenth century, it was listed as a real reptile. After this point it began to be classified as legendary. The basilisk or cockatrice is alleged to be very, very frightening. Reported to stand upright with the face of either a human or a cock, winged, with fowl feet and a serpent's tail, it can kill with a glance or even with its breath. The cockatrice is exactly the magical talisman needed to freeze any Internet enemy, virus, or technical complication dead in its tracks.

There are three ways that I know to go about creating a cockatrice. The first and most common method is for a toad or serpent to lie upon a cock's egg that is lying in dung or poisonous matter. This method of creation is the most difficult, as cocks' eggs are rather hard to come by. Hens' eggs absolutely will not do. The second method known is by planting a hair plucked from the head of a menstruating woman into a pot of soil. It is said that the cockatrice will then grow out of this soil. I recommend placing a small pot of soil on a windowsill or table near your main computer and burying a piece of hair within it. If you cannot fulfill this yourself, use a hair from a girlfriend, business partner, or employee. The third method of giving birth to a basilisk is actually too difficult to even go into, so I advise the second and easiest method to accomplish this task. You will know once the basilisk has been born as your powers of annihilation on the Net will increase. Just be advised to always keep your eyes open while on-line. According to legend, the cockatrice has two vulnerabilities: 1) It may be killed by someone who sees it before it sees him, and 2) beware the weasel. It is the only animal that can kill a cockatrice.

The dominatrix would also do well to create a cockatrice talisman, especially if her business increases by her being known as a femme fatale. It is actually believed that dread over this legendary monster stems out of ancient fear of woman's blood and its deadly power. Later medieval legends equate the femme fatale with the poison damsel, a woman who kills through the passing of venereal disease. If your work actually involves sexual intercourse, it would be inadvisable to create a cockatrice (very bad for business)! However, based on my interviews with over one hundred and fifty dominatrixes I have come to understand that their work is mostly psychological mind play with words and often does not even involve dressing up or any physical contact. In these cases, the cockatrice will help you instill deadly fear and command with your very first glance.

This leads me to another key element in common with the dominatrix and the Web designer. Both need to intuit what the client needs as quickly as possible. These professions both involve being somewhat of a mind reader. Following is a simple spell to help you read the thoughts of others.

Combine dried rosebuds, ginger powder, sweet basil, clove, cinnamon, vanilla, mint, and gold sparkles. The rose, basil, and vanilla are friendly herbs that relax and open up the minds of your clients. Ginger and cinnamon summon swiftness. Clove and mint give you mastery in all situations. The gold glitter or sparkles bring all things to light. All ingredients must be ground to a fine powder. This is an old witches' formula to open up your intuitive senses as well as give you mastery and control. Dust your hands and anoint your temples to help you quickly intuit and fulfill clients' needs.

WORK THE ZODIAC

No matter what sign you were born under, you can work the zodiac to magically enhance your career. The following twelve spells list some professions ruled by each sign as well as certain characteristics associated with the sign. Foods associated with each sign are also listed. I have tried to include what I feel are the most popular foods of each sign or those that will be easy to work into your weekly diet. Eat foods associated with your line of work in order to increase your chances for success in that field. Or eat foods to develop the characteristics of the sign, no matter what your line of work is.

I. Aries is the sign of the self-employed, military, the martial arts, or for anyone about to begin a new business or profession. Aries is the first sign of the zodiac and is used to initiate new beginnings and develop self-will. It is also the sign of leaders. Carrots, radishes, gingerbread, and mustard are all ruled by Aries.

2. Taurus is the sign for singers and bankers. It rules money, material possessions, earning power, security, and peace. Taurus foods include apples, avocado, spinach, sugar, tomatoes, and vanilla.

3. Gemini is for writers, reporters, and educators. It rules all forms of communication and information including writing, speech, phone, fax, E-mail, radio broadcasting, television, books, and newspapers. Short-distance travel, creativity, networking, and inspiration are also ruled by Gemini. Almonds, beans, parsley, and pasta are foods of the Twins.

4. Cancer is the sign of the mother and home. House-wives, interior decorators, real estate agents, or anyone who works out of the home can benefit from Cancerian energy. Laundry services and funeral homes are also associated with this sign. Qualities are shrewdness and nurturing. Crab, cucumber, potato, soup, and yogurt are some foods connected with this sign.

5. Leo is the sign of the actor, public speaker, and the gambler. The stock market, dating services, all professional sports, businesses connected with children or child education are also ruled by this sign. Popularity, drama, social success, and charisma can be summoned with chocolate, corn, olives, pineapple, raisins, or sunflower.

6. Virgo is the editor, researcher, doctor or health worker, psychoanalyst, and sous chef. Concentration, discrimination, practicality, efficiency, analysis, logic, and focus can be improved with the inclusion of barley, oat, rye, and/or salt in the diet.

7. Libra is the judge, lawyer, artist or art dealer, diplomat, and chef. Libra rules partnerships, contracts, agreements, public relations, commerce, and decision making. Bread, carob, granola, and wheat are foods of the Scales.

8. Scorpio rules the sex industry, spies, taxes, inheritance of property or money, insurance, funerals, wills, estate planning, corporate money, the occult, science, mathematics, and atomic physics. Wow! Scorpio traits are cunning, rejuvenation, intrigue, danger, and sex appeal. All spicy foods, and anything in the onion family (shallots, chives, scallions, leeks) will bring out the Scorpio sting.

9. Sagittarius is the professor, the philosopher, the rabbi, priest, or minister, and the travel agent. Long-distance travel, long-term goals, publishing, higher education, religion, philosophy, and foresight are all ruled by the Archer. Eat figs, drink root beer or tea to improve your aim.

10. Capricorn is the sign of government and corporate business. It rules power, ambition, status, politics, discipline, tenacity, endurance, stamina, completion of long-term goals, and professional and public reputation. Eat beets, aged cheeses, cranberry, and vinegar to climb like the Goat.

11. Aquarius is the inventor, the innovator, the electrician, the mason or architect. It is the sign of the humanitarian and rules teamwork or group energy. Drink beer or anything carbonated and add nuts to the diet to create more cooperation and free up your thinking.

12. Pisces is the poet, the dreamer, the mystic, and the ruler of hospitals, mental institutions, and monasteries. Qualities include solitude, wisdom, understanding, artistic creativity, and sensitivity. Pisces is also the sign of enemies, sacrifice, and self-undoing. Eat fish or shellfish to protect yourself from the unknown, the unconscious and hidden enemies. Sorbet can be eaten to enhance the positive qualities of Pisces.

The signs can also be combined to create certain effects. For example, Taurus provides security while Gemini opens creative channels. Apples and almonds or spinach pasta can be eaten to provide more creative ways to make money or to provide the freelancer with steady work. Taurus and Libra food combinations support commercial artistic success, whereas Pisces and Libra would be combined for the fine arts. I recommend Taurus/Leo food combinations for the opera singer or rock star. Virgo and Sagittarius combinations can be used for meticulous focus on the day-to-day tasks without losing sight of the long-range plans. Scorpio foods combined with any other sign will add more intrigue and Scorpio can be used to draw other people's money for investment. Be creative and work your own zodiac combinations.